The Faraway Horses

The Faraway Horses

The Adventures and Wisdom of One of
America's Most Renowned Horsemen

Buck Brannaman
with William Reynolds

Lyons Press
Guilford, Connecticut
An imprint of The Globe Pequot Press

Acknowledgments

A good idea for a book starts out like a young horse—lots of promise but it's all in the follow-through. Over the four years we've worked on this book, there have been some significant people who have entered our lives and given us counsel on this project. Special thanks goes to Betsy and Forrest Shirley, Tom Brokaw, Robert Redford, Patrick Markey, Bernie Pollack, Kathy Orloff, Donna Kail, Craig and Judy Johnson, Suzanne and Paul DelRossi, John and Jane Reynolds, Lindy Smith, Verlyn Klinkenborg, Chas Weldon, Joe Beeler, Elliott Anderson, Adrianne Fincham, Steve Price, and Jesse Douglas. At The Lyons Press, we thank Tony Lyons for seeing the vision and Ricki Gadler for putting up with us.

Our biggest thanks goes to the two women who believed in us all along—Mary Brannaman and Kristin Reynolds.

—Buck Brannaman and Bill Reynolds

Contents

Foreword

M Y "LIFE RELATIONSHIPS" with horses started after childhood, but I had wanted a pony as far back as I can remember. As a child of the 1950s and of a father who was a pioneer in television, I was never unaware of the impact of the TV western in my life. It fed my need for horseflesh at an addictive rate. This ultimately alarmed my parents. We were urban-bound and landlocked on three sides, so to slip a pony into the backyard would have been quite impossible without the fabric of the neighborhood coming apart at the seams. Of course, I knew and actually understood the problem, but I refused to let the pressure off my parents. They tried valiantly with riding lessons and trips to dude ranches during school vacations, but it was never enough.

My first horse, unlike the Will James book of the same name, arrived during my early twenties. She was a young liver chestnut Quarter Horse mare with a flaxen mane and tail and was, if in my eyes alone, perfect. I should have sensed some trouble when it took us three hours to load her into a neighbor's trailer. It required all sorts of ropes and pulleys, with lots of yelling and screaming, but we got her in. My adventure had begun.

* * *

I met Buck Brannaman in 1985. He was at a local arena in Malibu, California, and to see a Montana cowboy work with a bunch of hunter/jumper riders was a sight I didn't want to miss. I had heard a little bit about Buck from my friend Chas Weldon, the legendary saddlemaker in Billings, Montana. Chas spoke quite highly of him, and said he was designed to ride horses. When I first saw Buck, I knew Chas was right. Buck is three-quarters leg, the kind of rider who can touch his heels under the belly of a horse at the lope. I later found out that he was rather short going through high school, but grew a full six inches in his senior year, which landed him on the basketball team. Is he tall? The man could hunt geese with a rake.

The first time you see Buck ride is a moment of lasting impression. It isn't just the way he sits a horse, although that in itself is rather impressive. As he rides, he seems to disappear into the action. People speak of "becoming one with" something. Buck doesn't ride a horse, he merges with it. The essence of this merger is a friendly takeover.

I've seen him ride hundreds of different horses, and it happens every time. There is a moment when these two beings open doors to each other and communication happens.

He creates an environment—unique to each horse he rides—that enables the two of them to work together. It still astounds me every time I see him ride a new colt. Each one is different, each is unique, and that's how he treats them. If this sounds like a good way to be with people, you're catching on.

Buck has done more good for families, as well as their horses, than any man I know. He does this by getting people to slow down and listen: listen to their horses, their kids, their husbands, and their wives. He is about respecting others, whether they are people or horses—they're all the same to him.

THE FARAWAY HORSES opens a door into the life of Buck Brannaman. He has chosen to open it and let us all in. In his own words, he takes you through his difficult childhood and his youth growing up in a foster home. It is the story of a life of discovery, of pain and tragedy, and of finding one's way and then giving back to the ones who saved him. For Buck, it was horses. The horses saved his life.

These stories make up a significant young man's life, a young man who changes for the better the lives of every horse and rider he comes in contact with. I am proud to call him my friend and to have worked on this book. Quite simply, we need a lot more like him.

Bill Reynolds
Santa Ynez, California
2001

Introduction

THE STORIES IN THIS BOOK are scenes from the private movie of my life. They have helped me understand the big picture, and they have influenced directions I've taken since the events happened. In many ways they have affected the way I work with certain horses. I know they have influenced me in the way I deal with people, but horses have always meant a certain level of consistency in my life. They respond with all their being. All they know is honesty.

On my way to a horsemanship clinic I was putting on in Ellensburg, Washington, I decided to make a little detour through Coeur d'Alene, Idaho. It's a peaceful town, and its beauty is magnetic. I can see why so many people have come here to retire.

I sat looking out my truck window, with my horses standing quietly in my trailer, at the old house at 3219 North Fourth Street. That's where my older brother, Smokie, and I lived with our mom and dad for a few years in the mid-1960s. Seeing it more than thirty years later brought back a flood of memories.

The shed, not much more than an overhang to the back of the house, made me think of milking cows there, and how, in the eyes of a kid just four feet tall, that pitiful little shed seemed like a huge barn. When I saw the basement window, I remembered struggling to drag a hose through it so I could water our horses, cows, and pigs, and how more often than not that hose would hang up at the hose joint a few feet short of the stock tank.

The yard was where Smokie and I learned to ride and spin a rope, little knowing we would soon be performing on TV and at rodeos and fairs around the country as "The Idaho Cowboys, Buckshot and Smokie, from Coeur d'Alene, Idaho."

The number on that beat-up old mailbox stared back at me: 3219. I was tempted to knock on the door to see who lives there, and maybe walk around a little.

So many memories. So many times the ambulance would arrive at the house to collect my mom because she was having a diabetic reaction. And so many times our neighbors would call the sheriff because old man Brannaman was working his kids over again.

But today, I'm no longer afraid, not even of the memories. In a strange, almost melancholic way, it felt good to be here. Who would have thought that one of those "Idaho Cowboys" would grow up and have the joy of working with so many people and their horses, trying to help create relationships based on trust? It's ironic. Trust was something I had in short supply as a youngster.

Ride with me now, and I'll tell you some of what's happened along the way. It's been kind of bumpy, but well worth the trip.

Things are so good for me now due, in large part, to my wife, Mary. It is to her, to my family, and to the Horse that I dedicate not only this book, but my life.

Thank you for your interest, and may your life be filled with good horses.

Buck Brannaman
Sheridan, Wyoming
2001

1
Growing
Pains

I'M ABOUT HALFWAY THROUGH a year's worth of giving horse clinics around the country. I love what I do, but
I'm away from my family for long stretches at a time, and
that's tough. My wife, Mary, stays at our ranch with our three
daughters doing all the things a working ranch demands.
Leaving them is hard. My youngest daughter still asks, "Why,
Daddy, do you have to go and ride the faraway horses?"

So off I go for three to four days at each stop, meeting
people and their horses, helping them get along and get
things done together. Then I leave. I'm always starting, but
I'm always leaving. When the expressions of the horses and
the people start to become more pleasing to the eye, I have
to say so long.

It's hard to explain how other people's horses could save
your life, but that's exactly what happened to me. I've been
thinking about this quite a bit lately.

Today my horses and I rolled into a clinic in North Carolina. It's a fall day, and the sun is just up. It's just past that time in the early morning when you can close your eyes, turn around, and pinpoint the first fingers of the rising sun. I love that time. Everything starts fresh from that point on: the day, the horses, and the people. It's a quiet time, as well.

I talk all day for a living, so I do appreciate quiet. I get to feed and saddle horses in the quiet. The only sounds are those of the horses as they eat. There is a wonderfully predictable sameness to this scene, yet there is a newness that seems to permeate each first day of a clinic. I can feel the possibilities. It's a reassuring constant. The idea of constancy is something that I've valued ever since I was little, because it wasn't there much then.

I was born in 1962, in Sheboygan, Wisconsin, but I grew up in Idaho and Montana. My family lived in California for a little while, but by the time I was two years old we were living in the house on North Fourth Street in Coeur d'Alene, Idaho.

Given all that happened when I was little, the geography probably saved me as much as the horses did. The populations of Idaho and Montana are about the same as many small cities in this country, so you can imagine how small some of the towns in these states can be. Those stories you hear about towns being only "a bar and a post office" are true in many cases.

My dad, Ace Brannaman, was a talented man who had many jobs. He was a union cable splicer, and he worked on construction crews building steel towers carrying power lines from the hydroelectric dams that were being constructed across the West and up in Alaska. He had a saddle and boot repair shop, and he was a private security cop for a while. Then he worked in a sheriff's department as a deputy, which is kind of ironic when you look back at some of the things he did later on in his life.

My mom, Carol Alberta Brannaman, worked for General Telephone and Electric in Idaho, then as a waitress when we moved to Montana.

I went through a bunch as a little guy, and I can tell you there were times when I wondered if my brother and I would make it. I can remember looking up at the sky and, however simplistic it may seem now, wondering if there was a God up there. I'm sure at times we all ponder whether or not there's a God. I find myself asking "big" questions when I'm driving or riding alone on horseback, and I'm here to tell you there is a God; if you don't want to call Him that, call Him—or Her—what you want.

I was thinking about this quite a few years ago when Mom was still alive. She had diabetes, and it was real serious then. Medical science didn't have much luck controlling diabetes in those days, and even though she gave herself insulin shots, she'd been in and out of the hospital a number of times.

Dad was working in Alaska, and my older brother, Smokie, and I were at home in Coeur d'Alene with her. I was five years old, the same age as my daughter Reata is now. Late one night, Smokie and I heard something that woke us up. My mother was having a diabetic reaction, going through the stage of delirium that typically precedes a coma unless treatment is given right away. We ran into the bedroom, terrified. Mom was having a hard time. Smokie was only seven, and as he was trying to settle her, he hollered for me to run into the living room and call an ambulance.

I raced into the living room, but the phone was up on a railing, and I couldn't reach it. As I was scrambling up a chair back, the phone rang. I still couldn't reach it, so I grabbed a towel from the stove in the kitchen and snapped the receiver down from its perch. Scared that my mom was going to die, I yelled into the receiver, "I don't know who you are, but my mom's going to die if you don't help me. We need an ambulance because my mom's a diabetic." And then I stood up on the chair and hung it up.

The call had come from an old gentleman named Mr. Thompson. The Thompsons were probably the only black family in Coeur d'Alene in those days. Mr. Thompson had come to build a life for his family by running a dairy herd on the backside of Lake Coeur d'Alene. My dad had about seven years of vet school when he was a young man, and when he was home from a construction job, he ran sort of a black market veterinary service. He'd pull calves, and doctor cattle, and sew up horses for people. Mr. Thompson had called to have a calf pulled.

When I told Mr. Thompson to call the ambulance and then hung up, I had no idea who I was speaking to. Of course, he called the ambulance and sent it to our house, and within just a few minutes it arrived. The paramedics took my mother to the hospital, and Smokie and I were taken to the neighbors and stayed the night. After a few days of worry, my mom was home, and everything was fine again.

It was uncanny how the phone happened to ring just as I'd gotten to it. If I'd picked it up a second sooner, Mr. Thompson's call would have been cut off.

Timing is everything.

Timing was always a part of my young life. Timing and practicing. My entire youth was spent practicing. Not the piano or tennis, but rope tricks.

As a young man, my dad admired the famous trick roper Montie Montana, and he became infatuated with Montana's life. After returning from World War II, he realized he would never be a Montie Montana, but he decided that his boys would be. He would live vicariously through Smokie and me—Dad figured "Buckshot" and "Smokie" would sell better than Dan and Bill, so I became Buckshot and Bill became Smokie.

Dad pushed us real hard. My brother and I would practice for hours each day. We had the choice of practicing rope tricks or getting whipped. After just a few whippings, we sorted out pretty quick that practicing our rope tricks was the wise choice to make.

The reward was to travel around the country and perform. We all went as a family, and Mom would hover over us making sure life went on as normally as possible. Although I enjoyed the audience's applause and attention, there were days when we'd have given anything to go out and play baseball. We did a bit, but most days consisted of getting on a horse and practicing roping.

I learned to ride when I was three, about the same time I started practicing rope tricks. Dad got Smokie and me some gentle horses, put us on, and away we went, taking easy rides around the yard. My dad could ride a little bit, but he just didn't seem to have talent for working with horses. I wouldn't say that he was abusive, at least not all the time, but he didn't have feelings or compassion for horses. He was of the old school, like a lot of people were then, and looking back, I just don't think he knew a hell of a lot about horses. His folks were farmers—he had been raised on a farm in Indiana—so he never really learned much about working with horses.

Our first performance as trick ropers was two years later on a Spokane, Washington, TV talent show called the *Starlit Stairway*. It was on Channel 6 and was sponsored by Boyle Heating Oil. A couple of little girls sang the jingle for Boyle Heating Oil, and I thought they were the most beautiful girls I'd ever seen. Granted, I was only five or six years old, but I guess I must have had an eye for the ladies even then. I thought they were big stars because I'd see them every week on TV.

Buck practicing his blindfolded routine. This picture was fea-tured in a story about Buck and his brother that ran in the newspaper Montana Standard.

The talent was mostly local kids, tap dancing, singing, or playing musical instruments. During the auditions, there was a girl ahead of us tap dancing. She had her long blond hair all done up in curlers, and as she was dancing this little routine, the curlers started falling out of her hair almost in time with the music. I was just a little guy, and I thought that was the neatest thing. I couldn't imagine how they had done those curlers up so they could fall out in perfect time like that, and how she didn't run out of curlers until the dance was over. The girl was so embarrassed she started crying. I wondered why in the world she would be crying after such a nice performance.

When Smokie and I did our rope tricks, I had to stand on a box. I was a bit of a runt in those days, so my dad made a cube out of plywood and painted it white, and I stood on top of it. If I didn't, I was so short my rope would hit the ground when I spun it.

We did rope tricks like Wedding Rings, the Merry-Go-Round, Ocean Waves, and Texas Skips. During the commercial break, the judges were talking about who they were going to award first place. Our family was kind of huddled together, and I remember hearing the judges say, "Let's give it to those Idaho cowboys from Coeur d'Alene." And they did. They awarded us first prize for the talent show that night. I don't remember what the prize was, but the name "The Idaho Cowboys" stuck. From then on, we were billed as "The Idaho Cowboys, Buckshot and Smokie."

By the time I was six or seven, Smokie and I joined the Rodeo Cowboys Association, now called the Professional Rodeo Cowboys Association (PRCA), and had started performing at local rodeos around the country. Most of these shows were little "pumpkin rollers" that didn't amount to much, but they were a big deal to us.

A rodeo performance in Spanish Forks, Utah, in 1971. From left: Ace Brannaman, Buck, bullfighter Tim Oyler, and Smokie.

My dad changed jobs quite a bit during this period, but most of the time he was working for himself in his saddle and boot repair shop. He worked around our roping career so he could haul us to rodeos. The money that we made all went into his pocket, so the trick roping was kind of his job, too, or so he looked at it.

Our mom was quite a seamstress. She'd buy material and make us flashy outfits like the singing cowboys used to wear on stage and in the movies. I still have some of them. Other than a couple of pictures and some really nice memories, they're all I've got left of her. I wish I could have known her as an adult.

In 1969, Smokie and I performed at our first indoor rodeo, a big one called the Diamond Spur Rodeo in Spokane, Washington. We had done trick roping at quite a few amateur rodeos, and we were getting to where we were fairly well known in northern Idaho and eastern Washington, but we were just starting our professional careers elsewhere.

It was a Thursday, the opening night of the rodeo. I looked into the coliseum from the back gate and saw eight thousand people in the grandstands. It was the biggest crowd I had ever seen, and I was very nervous. There were horses of every color moving in and out—it seemed like chaos at the time—but everyone knew where they were going. For a little kid who had barely been outside the Idaho panhandle, it was an amazing spectacle.

The rodeo clowns were getting their jalopy-car act prepared near one gate, while the barrel racers were blasting up and back along one of the handling chutes. Then the announcer started giving his introductions for the evening performance, and through all the confusion I heard, "Ladies and Gentlemen, The Idaho Cowboys!"

The plan was that Smokie and I would gallop into the arena on our pintos, make a full circle, do a sliding stop in the center, and then stand up on our horses and begin spinning ropes. When we made our grand entry, I had no time to be scared. Smokie took off first. He tipped his hat and made his circle, and I was right behind him. I got about a quarter of the way around when my mare Ladybird decided she was going to save us a lot of time. Evidently she thought making a full lap was pointless. She cut hard to her left and took me right out toward the center of the arena.

I was pulling as hard as a seven-year-old could pull. My brother looked across the arena at me, wondering what in the world I was doing while I looked right back at him wondering what I was going to do. About the time I got to the center of the arena, Ladybird slammed on the brakes and ejected me over her head. The world seemed to disappear as I did a complete somersault in the middle of the arena, then darned if I didn't land on my feet. And not only did I land on my feet, but I still had my rope in my hands. I stood there completely bewildered, amazed that I wasn't dead. I looked up at a now dead-silent crowd for about two seconds, and then began spinning my rope. My legs were shaking like Elvis doing "Blue Suede Shoes."

The crowd went nuts. Little did they know I had fallen in you know what and had come out smelling like a rose. Smokie couldn't believe it. I'm sure that seeing me fly through the air, he felt he was going to be the sole heir to the vast Brannaman family fortune of nine milk cows with pitifully small udders.

Every night from then on, the crowd would whisper in anticipation of this brilliant gymnast/trick roper who was only seven years old and could jump off a galloping horse at thirty-five miles an hour, do a flip in the air, land on his feet, and do rope tricks.

I never did that little trick again. It's funny how once in a while things can really go wrong yet they work out right in

Buck working his rope and the crowd at a Special Olympics demonstration in Butte, Montana.

spite of you. I've done a lot of things in life that have worked out in spite of me, but I'll never forget the Diamond Spur Rodeo, and how one of the best performances of my life was an accident.

Smokie and I had chores to do at home, including milking a handful of cows every morning and night. We had a milking machine, which sounds as if it would have made the work easier, but it was a two-boy job carrying all that milk to the house a tub at a time. Afterward we had to run all the milk through an old-fashioned cream separator. The separator had about two hundred parts, and we had to sterilize each one of them every single time we ran milk through it. That was quite a job because we milked those cows every day and night. Maybe that's why I don't drink milk anymore—I figure it might give relief to some poor little kid not to have to produce milk for me.

In the evenings after we finished milking, we'd practice our rope tricks. Smokie was a better roper than I was in those days. He could do the Texas Skip better than I could because he was taller and it was easier for him to jump through a vertical loop. But he didn't like to practice quite as much as I did, so when we were little guys, if he wasn't playing the games I wanted to play, I'd threaten to go practice my rope tricks. And if he wasn't practicing when I was, well, that was a good way to get a whipping from Dad for not putting out enough effort. That's the secret of how I could pretty much get Smokie to play whatever I wanted to.

We had a little round Black Angus bull we used to breed a bunch of milk cows with. Sampson was his name. He liked to hang around us, and he became pretty friendly.

When my paint mare, Ladybird, the horse I did rope tricks off of, became pregnant and I couldn't ride her, I got Sampson broke to ride. I had a heck of a time keeping the saddle on him (the bovine mouth isn't exactly designed for a snaffle bit), and Sampson kept rubbing the headstall off.

Still, everything worked out fine. I trained Sampson so he'd bow down to let me climb on and off, which became important because I was small in stature and Sampson kept growing. I'd take him up in the mountains, and even after Ladybird had her foal, I kept riding him.

Buck performing blindfolded atop Ladybird at the Diamond Spur Rodeo in Spokane, Washington.

I'd been riding Sampson for nearly a year and a half when my dad butchered him.

Dad didn't even warn me. It was as though he saw no need to talk to me about whether killing my pet was okay in my mind. It just happened. And what's more, he made my brother and me help.

Of course it affected me, but with my father you knew better than to show you were upset. To have shown any emotion would have upset my dad, and he would have taken it out on me.

So my dad made us help butcher my friend. And I ate Sampson, too, because I didn't want to suffer the consequences of not eating him.

Lots of things happen to little kids, but that's the sort of thing you never forget.

By the time I was eight, we had moved from Coeur d'Alene to Whitehall, Montana. Dad rented a Quonset hut with a brick front on Main Street and opened a saddle and repair shop. My mom worked in a restaurant about fifty miles away in a little town called Ennis.

Smokie and I walked home from school for lunch every day. After we ate Mom would take us back to school on her way to work. This meant in the afternoons, we'd be coming home from school to spend a few hours with Dad, without Mom around, after he got home from the repair shop.

When she dropped us off at school, I'd tell her how scared I was to be home alone with Dad. I was afraid of doing something wrong, afraid of getting whipped. Smokie was a little tougher and had a thicker hide, but I was Mom's baby. I'd beg her not to leave me, and every day she'd cry.

I never really considered how hard that was on her, but I knew how hard it was on me. I was terrified. I hated for lunchtime to come. It seems funny that a little boy would be afraid of lunch coming, but that's what lunchtime signified to me every day, five days a week. I was afraid to go home. I was terrified of my dad. For no reason Smokie and I could figure out, he was always angry. Whatever the reason, Dad was an angry man. There were days when he would come home and just beat us. He'd whip us with belts or riding quirts or anything handy, but always when Mom was gone. She never would have allowed it if she'd been around. She was our protector, but we were afraid to tell her.

My folks did really love each other. Dad always drank some, but he wasn't a real problem drinker while Mom was alive. He always had kind of a mean side to him, and it didn't take drinking for it to come out. It was pretty much out all the time. We didn't know the way he treated us was called abuse, because we'd never known anything else. It wasn't life-threatening, at least not until after Mom died, but it was damn sure cruel.

Nowadays Dad would have gotten in trouble with the law for what he was doing, but back then law enforcement didn't have much to do with domestic problems. Besides, most people didn't know what was going on. If I saw someone now treating his young boys the way Dad treated us, I think I might have to work him over.

When I was a kid, I always wondered why my mom didn't leave and take us boys with her, but in those days it wasn't acceptable to leave a marriage. She wasn't raised that way. Her parents were German immigrants who wouldn't have thought very much of her if she hadn't been able to tolerate even a bad marriage. It was a different time, and they would have blamed her, not Dad.

I know she hated for lunchtime to come, too, because she'd have to say good-bye, and by the time she finished cleaning up the restaurant and got home, it would be late at night. Some days things were okay with Dad. He didn't give us a hard time. But there were a lot of days when he'd holler at us, and we'd get whipped. It's not that Mom didn't know. I suppose she always knew what kind of man Dad was.

There's something that kicks in when a mother sees her children being abused. Maternal instinct takes over, and she can fight like a lion. But Mom was in a bad spot. Strong as she was, she felt trapped. She had no way to make enough money to support three of us, nowhere to go, and she was a long way from her family. I'm sure she could have given a hundred reasons why she stayed married. Maybe some of it was denial. Maybe she just didn't want to believe that she'd made such a bad choice. There are a lot of things about my mom's past that made her what she was, things I'll never know, and if she were still alive, there are a lot of questions I would love to ask her.

There was an afternoon that we came home from school when Mom was at work, and Dad was moving around, walking around the place, going in and out of the barn. I knew he was mad. It was only about a hundred yards from the county road to the house, and I wished we could take all night to get there. When he saw us, he immediately started hollering and swearing. One of us had left a gate open when we were doing chores in the morning. You know young boys, you know how forgetful they can be. They don't mean to do anything wrong—a lot of times they just forget, or something makes their brains turn off.

Anyhow, we'd left a gate open. Nothing really had gone wrong. One of our horses got into a pen with another horse, but they were geldings and they got along fine. It was really no big deal, just a matter of catching the horse and putting him back in his own pen. But Dad was so angry that we had forgotten to close the gate that he went into the barn and came out with his stock whip. The whip was eight feet long. I knew what was coming, and my little legs were just shaking.

He told us to put our books down on the front steps. We were on the east side of the house in the backyard near Mom's clothesline. I was wearing a short-sleeve shirt and a pair of lightweight pants. I remember looking at those clothes on the clothesline and wishing I had them all on at the same time to protect me from what was about to happen.

Dad made us go over to a rail fence that ran around the house. He told us to hang on to one of the rails and stand there, and then he started whipping us with that stock whip. Once in a while the lash would wrap around my arm up by my shoulder, and it'd crack just like a .22 rifle. It hurt as if I had been shot, too. There were even places where it cut through my shirt. Granted, it probably wasn't much of a shirt, but still, whipping a kid hard enough to cut his shirt meant you were hitting him pretty hard.

Dad was whipping us over our backs and down our legs when I saw a neighbor looking out of his ranch house at us. He didn't know what to do, but I remember looking at him and wishing he was man enough to come over and stop what was happening.

My dad was still hollering, cussing, and whipping us when the phone rang. He told us to stay where we were and ran into the house to answer it. When he came back out, his mood had changed. The phone call was from someone who wanted Smokie and me to do a TV commercial for Kellogg's Sugar Pops. Dad was excited now. This was another chance for him to vicariously share the spotlight with us. He went from whipping us to being as happy as could be. At the time, we didn't give a damn about a TV commercial, but we sure were glad the phone rang when it did.

I've often thought it was by the grace of God that the phone rang that day and cut our whipping short, or we'd have gotten it a lot worse than we did. We went ahead and made the Sugar Pops commercial. The funny thing was they shot it in a town called Grace, Idaho. You know, there are so many little coincidences in life that make you wonder how God or your guardian angel or whoever it is protecting you can keep it all straight. You start putting all those pieces together years later, and it's kind of surreal.

* * *

When I was eleven and we were living in Whitehall, Mom had a bad bout of the flu. She'd been in bed for two or three days, and Dad was trying to take care of her. When he gave her some soup, it never occurred to any of us that the soup would change her blood sugar level. During the night, she went into a diabetic coma, although nobody knew it. The next morning, Dad was worried. He came in, woke us up, and said, "We have to take your mother to the hospital in Ennis."

Mom was a big lady, all of six feet tall, and it took all three of us to get her into the truck. She was in terrible distress, and she couldn't control her bladder. Dad and Smokie held her upper body to help her into the truck. I grabbed her legs and carefully lifted them in. Urine ran down over my hands. That really scared me. I knew Mom was bad. I knew it was awfully serious.

Dad left us at home, took off with Mom for the hospital, and we went on to school. We worried about our mother all day and all night, but Dad never called. Mom was in the hospital for three long days, and during that entire time we never heard from him.

Finally, on the morning of the fourth day, Dad came home. He just came into the house and stood before us, and said, "Boys, your mother's gone."

That was it. I was shocked. Mom had been in and out of the hospital so many times with her diabetes that I figured she'd come home, and we'd go on. But she didn't, and we had to.

* * *

For Mom, trick roping had meant more than anything. It was the glue that held our family together. When Smokie and I did the Sugar Pops commercial, she loved it. The spot ran nationally, and we were dubbed "The Sugar Pops Kids." Mom's only moment in the limelight had been as a dance instructor at an Arthur Murray dance studio when she was a young woman, and she was elated that we were on national television. She would sit in front of the TV and pray that the commercial would come on.

After Mom passed away, one of her nurses who went to the funeral told me that while she had been in a coma the entire time she was in the hospital, they had left a TV playing in her room. I guess they thought the constant voices and sounds would help stimulate her back to consciousness. Just before she died, our Sugar Pops commercial came on and Smokie and I were doing our rope tricks. As soon as the commercial was over, Mom passed away.

I can't help but think that she heard our voices, and maybe that was all she needed. Maybe hearing her babies one last time was her way of saying good-bye. I guess we all have our way of saying "I love you and good-bye." Timing again. It just keeps showing up.

With Mom gone, Dad changed for the worse. He had always been pretty rough on us, and it had gotten to the point where he'd been turned in to the law quite a few times, but he never did anything life-threatening while Mom was alive. The moment he told us she was gone, I knew life was going to get tougher.

Within a year of Mom's death, Dad had pretty much fallen apart. He really loved Mom, and losing his wife seemed to drive him over the brink. He drank heavily, and he just didn't want to live anymore. He'd had a rough life. He had been a prisoner of war in Germany for over a year during World War II. God knows what they did to him— he never told us—but maybe he never got over the experience. To make matters worse, Dad had a near-fatal accident in Alaska, receiving a big jolt of electricity while working as a lineman. He was in the hospital for six or eight months. After he came home, he suffered from horrible headaches. They seemed to torture him for the rest of his life.

Ace Brannaman provided for his boys however he could. Here he arrives home with a poached antelope.

For whatever reason he justified his anguish by blaming Smokie and me. Maybe he thought that if we weren't around, Mom would still be alive. Not our mom, mind you, his wife.

During that time, Smokie and I would talk as we walked to the bus stop for school, pondering whether or not we were going to live through the next night, let alone the school year. We lived in fear every day. We felt we had no safe place and were heading down a road with no good ending in sight.

Dad was drinking so much he couldn't sleep. It got to where he would keep us awake many nights running, hollering and screaming at us, beating us, and slapping us around. Our dining room table was solid oak and surrounded by oak captain's chairs. I stared at that wood grain a lot when he made us sit there and take his yelling.

By the time he was thoroughly liquored up, it would be late. The woodstove in the corner would have long gone out, and the house would have turned cold. Dad would get us out of bed, and we'd have to sit there in our underwear, shaking from the cold and knowing what was ahead of us. He'd never notice our discomfort or fear because he was so full of his own "antifreeze."

One night Dad pulled us out of bed about midnight. He'd been on a drinking binge since shortly after dinner. We had to sit down at the table while he yelled at us for a couple of hours. It must have been two or three o'clock in the morning, and we begged him to let us go back to bed.

But no. He walked from the table to the refrigerator, reached in the freezer, and pulled out one of his trusty bottles of vodka. He'd drink some of that and then he'd drink a beer. It was his ritual. On his return from the kitchen he'd ask us, "What are you little bastards looking at?" That was the tip-off. Another butt-whipping party was about to start, and we were the guests of honor.

Dad had a riding crop with a molded plastic handle that he'd use on us (I'm sure that's the reason why even today I'm still a little touchy about riding crops). We were too afraid to run because Dad always told us we'd get it worse if we did. But this night he was really drunk, and we couldn't face it. We'd had enough. We were tired of going to school bruised and beaten and with no sleep, so we took off running.

The house was perfect for a chase. It had a sort of island in the middle, and a full circle would take you from the kitchen through the bathroom, into the living room and dining room, and back again.

We ran through the kitchen. I was in the lead, with Smokie right behind me. Dad was on the other side of the house trying to catch up. Suddenly Smokie stopped, opened the drawer where the cutlery was kept, and pulled out a steak knife. The desperate look in his eyes scared me, but I understood. Smokie just didn't want another beating. He was finally going to take care of us.

I knew that if Dad saw him with that knife, Smokie would have to use it, because if he didn't, Dad would take it away from him and kill him with it. I collected every last bit of calm I had left in me, and quietly whispered, "Smokie, please put that knife back in the drawer. Don't let him see it."

Smokie paused just for a moment. It's almost as if God kept my dad out of sight long enough for Smokie to put that knife back in the drawer.

We couldn't have looked at each other for more than a half second, but it's a moment we will remember for the rest of our lives.

Dad caught Smokie and started beating him. "Dad, please," I begged, "please don't. Please don't hurt him."

Dad looked at me and he said, "You get off of my ass."

I don't know why, but I said, "I'm not on your ass."

That was a big mistake. The words pulled Dad off my brother; he came after me, and he had me cornered. The only way out was through the front door, and I made a mad dash for it. For some reason Dad didn't follow me. Too drunk, I guess.

It was the middle of the winter, with snow on the ground and a temperature of ten below zero. Outside, standing there in my underwear, I had very few choices.

The best choice involved my bloodhound, Duke. Duke lived out in the yard, in a fifty-five-gallon barrel with a bunch of straw in it. He weighed about 110 pounds, way more than I did, but I crowded into the barrel with him, huddling beside him. Duke kept me warm, for otherwise I would surely have frozen to death.

Duke and I stayed in that barrel for a couple of hours, and then I began to worry. Was Smokie okay in there?

Would he be dead when I came in? If he was, would Dad kill me, too? Although those are hardly thoughts any little boy should have, I had them. And I didn't know what to do.

Finally, even in spite of Duke, the cold just got too much for me, and I ventured back into the house. Luckily, Dad had so much liquor in him that when I came back in, he just looked at me and asked, "Where you been?" He'd already forgotten.

Smokie was all right. By that time Dad had had enough to drink so that when we again asked him if we could go to bed, he let us.

We got only a couple hours sleep before we had to go to school, but all things considered—and I know this sounds like the ultimate in denial—that night worked out pretty well compared to what could have happened.

Mom had been gone for about a year when Dad placed an ad for a maid in *Western Horseman* magazine. He really wasn't looking for a maid, he was looking for a date. And he found one: a lady named Norma moved out from Indiana with her boy, Tom, a nice kid about my age. It wasn't too long before Dad had married her, or at least that's what he told us. In any case, Norma wasn't a maid. She was more like a bed partner to him and sort of an imitation mom for Smokie and me.

For two or three months Dad was on good behavior. He didn't want Norma to think that he was anything like what he really was. Then after a while he felt less inhibited around her, and the drinking got worse again.

One night Dad got mad. It's hard to say about what, because usually it wasn't about anything that a sane person could understand. He kept us up, hollering and screaming and cussing at us. Norma went to bed. I could tell she was real worried for Tom, wondering what she'd gotten herself into.

Dad hadn't beaten us since Norma had been in the house, but that night he did. After he beat Smokie with that famous little riding crop, he turned it around to use the handle like a billy club and worked him over some more. Then he started slapping and punching me. I huddled down with my head mashed in a corner of the room. Dad had the heel of his boot on my throat, and he held a frying pan in his hand. I know Smokie would have helped me, but there wasn't a whole lot left of him after Dad had beaten him senseless.

I'll never forget the look on Dad's face as he screamed, "I'll fucking kill you, you little son of a bitch."

Although Dad beat the hell out of me, too, he didn't use the frying pan on me. He was too drunk to pick me up; he would have fallen on me if he'd tried. That's probably the only thing that stopped him.

Norma, who had heard all this going on, wasn't going to take the chance that Tom would be beaten or killed by this man whom she had misjudged. She made plans to leave the first chance she got.

She also talked to Johnny France, a deputy sheriff in Madison County, Montana. Now, some of the teachers at school knew what was going on. Smokie's physical ed teacher, Bob Cleverly, had seen the marks on him, and when he heard about what had happened, he, too, went to Deputy France. In

those days it wasn't really acceptable for law-enforcement officials to deal with family problems, but between Norma and
the teachers, everybody started trying to figure out a way to
get us out of there.

Dad was off at work, and Smokie, Tom, and I were at
home with Norma when she decided the time had come.
She was going to get Tom, who was more scared than he'd
ever been in his life, out of there, and she wanted Smokie
and me to go with them.

We were terrified to stay, but we were also terrified by the
thought of leaving. Dad was the only family we knew. But
when Norma assured us, "I'll take care of you boys. You can
come live with me, and I'll raise you like my own sons," she
convinced us to go.

Norma put us in her car and took us to a dumpy motel in
Ennis. It was one of those places where you pay by the
month and where the cockroaches can ground tie. Everything seemed to be going fine, or at least Smokie and I
thought so, but by the end of the week, the reality of raising
three boys by herself was more than Norma could handle,
and she decided she didn't want to keep us after all.

Norma put us back in the car, dropped us off at Deputy
France's house in Ennis, and drove away.

Talk about feeling lost and abandoned. Smokie and I had
really believed we were going to stay with Norma. Instead,
we found ourselves wards of the court and the responsibility
of the county.

We stayed with Johnny France in Ennis for a couple of
weeks. With the help of a social worker named Emery

Smith, we looked into living with a friend of our family who lived in California, a woman named Anne Annis who was sort of like an aunt to us. She and her husband had already raised a couple of kids of their own. They were just leaving for a month's vacation, so they couldn't take us right away.

Johnny France had had a tough time as a boy, too. When he wound up with no place to live and no family to take care of him, a couple named Forrest and Betsy Shirley took him in and raised him on their ranch near Norris. Johnny called the Shirleys and asked if we could stay for a month if we worked on the ranch. They thought that would be fine.

By the end of that month Smokie and I really cared for the Shirleys. Forrest was what I had always wished my dad could have been. And just before we were to leave, we asked them if there was some way we could stay. We liked being at the ranch. Anne Annis and her husband lived in a town in California, and if we moved in with them we'd never get to be around horses or cattle again, or be able to rope and ride and be cowboys like we wanted to be.

Forrest and Betsy said we could stay there and live with them. They became our foster parents, and their ranch became our home.

Dad was very bitter toward us after we left, and we had to go to court to get the few things that we owned: a couple of horses, a saddle or two, and our clothing. Forrest helped us through the court process, and the county appointed us an attorney to represent us. We won in court and got our belongings, but then—I'm not sure how it worked—I had my first lesson in how the legal system operated: we got a bill for $1,100 from our attorney. He told us he'd put a lien on our stuff if we didn't pay it. This guy was strong-arming his own clients, twelve- and fourteen-year-old boys.

So we sold what we had, the horses and the saddles and the rest of it, and we paid him off. We wound up with nothing, but the attorney got his money.

For the next several years, we would get birthday cards from Dad telling us that he was going to kill us when we turned eighteen. I don't know why eighteen was a significant number, but he told us that when we got to be eighteen, we weren't going to be around anymore. And he'd send us letters telling us that he'd been watching us from the ridgetop through his rifle scope, that he'd been watching our foster parents, too, and that he could take us all out any time he wanted.

Forrest took these threatening cards and letters to the sheriff, and finally the sheriff ran Dad out of the state. He told him that if he ever came back he'd put him in jail. These days, they'd probably react a little more strongly than they did then; they'd probably lock him up and throw away the key. As it was, Dad moved to Oregon, where he lived off his military pension and some other money from the power-line accident.

* * *

Several years later, after I'd gone to work as a cowboy for the Madison River Cattle Company, I wrote Dad a letter. I told him that I knew he was starting to get some age on him and that he might not live much longer. I wanted him to know that I still loved him because he was my father, no matter what had happened or what he had said and done to us. I didn't want him to die feeling like I hated him.

In the letter he wrote back, he seemed relieved. He didn't feel like I hated him, and I didn't.

I wouldn't say Dad spent the rest of his life a happy man. He lost all those years that he could have been with his boys, seeing us grow up and become men and then become husbands and fathers ourselves. But that was not his way.

That wasn't the way Smokie felt either. After we left the courtroom, Smokie never spoke to Dad again. I tried to get him to talk to him, but it was not in Smokie's personality. He would become curious at times over the years about what was going on with Dad, but he'd been hurt too much to make contact. And I think that was the right thing for Smokie. He and Dad might not have gotten along the second time around, either.

2
The
Buckskin
Gloves

I TRY TO GIVE THE HORSES I work with a safe place to be and a sense of peace. Sometimes this means their just standing near me for a quiet moment. The feeling may not hold long because trust doesn't just happen, but I know the horses feel the peacefulness. I felt it that night in the backyard when I was crammed into the barrel with my dog Duke. For a little while I was in a safe place for the first time since my mom died—a little cold, but safe.

I can't help remembering this time spent with Duke when it's time to wean our young colts. We wean them when they're six months old, and no matter how many years I work with horses, I still feel sympathy for the youngsters. I know the terror that must well up in them when we separate them from their mothers, and I try to make being weaned as easy for them as I can.

The colts make a clean break from the mares. I like to take the colts out of earshot, so the mares don't hear their cries and become frantic. Mothers love their babies, and it's hard on them, too.

The first few months of life are a very precious time for the foal and the mare. The mare's instincts have evolved over thousands of years, and she knows more about her baby's needs and comfort level than I do. My colts end up being comfortable with my presence and handling after I wean them.

The first few days of separation are a troubling time for these young horses. It's therefore necessary that they have the chance to work things out for themselves. Quite often the colts take support from one another because we leave them together as a herd. To further help the process along, I always put a "baby-sitter" in with the newly weaned colts, usually an older retired gelding whose stability is reassuring to the little ones. This isn't an idea I came up with on my own—people have been doing it for years, but because of what I went through as a kid, I know what it feels like to have my mother taken away. I understand the reassurance and comfort that can come from a stabilizing factor.

The colts get along well with the gelding. In the beginning he's a calming influence. Later on he provides discipline within the group, which helps keeps delinquency to a minimum.

We leave the youngsters alone at first. They need to be with other weanlings and their "baby-sitter" without being disturbed. You're not going to teach them a whole lot while they're troubled and insecure. But if you give them time to settle themselves before you begin halterbreaking them, there is a good chance these young horses won't become herdbound or socially bankrupt. They'll get from you what you are responsible for giving: guidance, teaching, and a safe place to be.

We begin working with the babies at the point when they are peaceful and beginning to be relaxed about not being nursed by their mothers. We give them the gift of time. This is something every baby deserves—horse or human. It's the time when we start a lifelong relationship with the babies. We replace their mothers, and they place their lives in our hands. I view this as an honor and privilege as well as a responsibility.

The first order of business when I work with a young horse is to replace that awful void created by separation from his mother. She's no longer there as a friend and, most important, as a leader. Leadership is what his mother had to offer. Hopefully, a young horse gets it from a good human, but, unfortunately, that's where humans often fall short.

After a day or two, when the colts' cries for their mothers begin to subside, we start halterbreaking them. We work the colts on the end of a halter rope, driving them around a round pen. We help them operate without being afraid, learning how to be led, or guided, by a human the same way their mothers led them. The colts don't begin by viewing humans the same way they did their mothers, but in time they can if a human offers support and not just affection.

Did you ever wonder how a mare can get her colt to follow regardless of whether he's hungry or not? She doesn't own a halter or rope, and she doesn't pull on him or otherwise force him to submit. Instead, she uses the herding instinct in both herself and her colt. She gets behind him and nudges his hindquarters—a little on the right, a little on the left—and all with just a gentle touch of her nose. Once the colt's feet are moving, she slips in front in order to "draw" his energy with her.

This technique is very useful in a variety of circumstances. You don't have to pull or try to dominate. You can put pressure on without being domineeringly physical. Once you've created the energy, you can then draw it in the direction you want to go. Subtle actions can have great effects, and believe it or not, some of this herding instinct remains in us humans, too.

Young children have little control over what happens to them. However, becoming adults gives them an opportunity to put things together and become sure of themselves. Many of you probably had some sort of black mark on your life when you were a youngster. You may have been abused or abandoned, but if as an adult you use these experiences to justify some proclaimed inadequacies, then you've made a mistake and missed some opportunities.

Adults are given free choice. When you grow up, you can't blame your inadequacies on your father for having been mean to you, for having whipped you, or on your mother for having been mean to you, or on anything else done by your aunt, or your uncle, or your grandparents. You have to take responsibility for what you are and where you're headed.

Horses are different from humans. We have to take responsibility for horses simply because they're always in our care. They can't get along without us. They're forced to live in our world. That's why the rules have changed: an adult horse in our world is still our responsibility. This doubles the burden for us humans. A human must be responsible for himself and for his horse. And when you succeed in both of those areas, life will be pleasant for you as well as for everyone around you.

In all the years that I've been giving clinics, I've heard a lot of people talk about how their horses have been abused. After they've told me all the things that a horse does and doesn't do for them, they'll tell me how they've rescued him. Sometimes these people sound as if they've started making excuses for the inevitable failures they have already mapped out for themselves. It's almost as if they feel that, having saved an abused horse, it's all right for them to fail at their horse work because, in their own minds, at least, they've been Good Samaritans.

However, many of these horses haven't been abused at all. They may have been neglected, or they may not have a lot of quality, or they may have lacked an adequate education, but they haven't been abused.

When it comes to a horse that truly has been abused, there are some things you need to understand. You can't cure what's wrong with him by just being sympathetic. You can't help him by just leaving him be and doing nothing.

That holds true for all abused creatures, as I found out about myself.

Some people think that the foster child program is always a bad situation. Well, let me tell you, it's not. Some really good people out there have put a lot of children's lives back together, with many happy endings.

After Mom was gone, our life with Dad got worse by the day. I'm sure if we'd been around another six months, one or both of us would have died, because Smokie was getting to the point where he wasn't going to take it much longer. Every day on the way home from school, we'd walk along the creek bottom that wound through the willows about a mile from the house in Whitehall, and we'd wonder if we were going to be around to make the same walk the next day, or if we were going to die at the hands of our father. The action that Johnny France took turned out to be the turning point in our lives.

Forrest and Betsy Shirley lived on a ranch outside Norris, just down the road from Bozeman. In addition to having raised four kids of their own, they had also provided a home for seventeen foster boys. Some stayed just for a short time, others for longer periods. Johnny France had been the first, and Smokie and I were the last. After we left, they didn't take in any more. I think they either figured they'd done a good job and weren't going to do any better, or we soured them on the deal altogether.

When Emery Smith, the social worker, dropped Smokie and me off at the Shirleys, we were a little scared. We were weary of dodging fists, belts, riding crops, and bowling trophies, and we weren't sure what life had in store for us at this point.

Forrest had gone to Billings for a day or two, and only Betsy was at home. She was a tiny woman, but she was full of love, and she swept us into our new life. The first night we were there, everybody was watching TV in the living room. There was another foster kid named Joe, a cowboy named Royce who had been a foster kid and worked at the ranch now, and Betsy and some of her friends. The TV was blaring, Smokie and Joe were talking, and the adults were visiting. I was so exhausted I lay down on an old knotty pine bench and used a stack of Navajo blankets as a pillow. I looked over the side of the bench and found myself staring into the mouth of an old metal spittoon. All the visiting cowboys used it, and the most awful smell you could imagine filled my little corner of the room. I sat up, carefully pushed the spittoon toward Joe with the toe of my boot, and lay back down.

I closed my eyes and felt for the first time in a long time that I wasn't going to be hurt. No matter how uncomfortable that little bench was, I felt at peace. No one was going to bother me. No one was going to stumble into my room drunk and holler at me, or make me get out of bed and sit at the dining room table in my underwear and listen to ranting and raving all night long. Spittoon and all, it was a very special night, and I carry it with me to this day.

The next morning, Smokie and I went down to help with chores at the barn. I just happened to be standing in the parking area by the ranch house when Forrest pulled in. I'd been wondering all morning what this man would be like and how he would treat Smokie and me. He'd been told what we had gone through, and I wondered if he was going to be sympathetic or uncomfortable and not know what to say. Was he not going to acknowledge us, or was he going to be mean to us like other men had been in the past?

Forrest got out of his truck and said, "You must be Buck."

I just nodded. I couldn't get any words to come out. My little legs were shaking. I was all of four-eleven and weighed eighty-seven pounds soaking wet. Forrest was six-four and had hands as big as those of any man I'd ever seen. He was a little wrinkled and old looking, but he still looked very strong.

Forrest walked toward me, and then, as if he had forgotten something, he turned on his heel and went back to his truck. When he reached into the front seat, I felt like a horse who'd been whacked too many times. What's he reaching for? I wondered.

It was a pair of buckskin gloves. Forrest tossed them to me and said, "You're gonna need these."

The gloves fit me perfectly. They had that wonderful smell of new leather and were as soft as the skin on a foal's nose. I couldn't look at Forrest. I just couldn't seem to process this simple act of kindness. Looking down at those gloves, considering the offering, I felt like a colt, confused and uncertain.

Forrest pointed to an old ranch truck and told me to get in with him. The truck bed was loaded down with fencing tools. Later on, I found out that Forrest always kept it loaded that way just in case he happened to have some company coming by for a free meal—he'd get a day's work out of them first.

I crawled up into the front seat, and off we went to one of the far corners of the ranch. There Forrest showed me how to patch fence by stretching wire and driving staples. Fixing seventy-five-year-old barbed-wire fence turned out to be quite a job. About the time we'd get a wire tight—*ping!*—it would break ten feet away.

I was so proud of those gloves, it was kind of hard getting much work out of me. I didn't want the barbs to tear them up. But work I did, and that afternoon in the pasture was a day that remains etched in my mind. It was a strangely comfortable time, filled with the smells of sage, lupine, and an occasional whiff of Forrest's cigar.

We went out for hours that day and just fixed fence, stretched wire, and put in posts. Forrest never really said much to me about where I'd come from or what I'd been through, and I was so happy he didn't. He just gave me something to do. He treated me as if I'd always been there, and I appreciated that.

I never realized at that age how wise he was, but I'm sure Forrest had put a lot of thought into his actions. We spent quite a few days together before he said much to me at all. And finally, around the time I was thinking, I wish he'd talk to me a little bit, he did just that. That's where his influence really began with me.

I would give anything to still have that pair of buckskin gloves. I don't know what ever happened to them, but I'll never forget them or what they represented. I could buy a hundred pairs right now and they wouldn't mean a thing to me, not like that pair did.

Smokie and I worked hard for Forrest, and he appreciated our effort. Deep down he felt sorry for us because of what we had gone through, but he was never overly sympathetic, and he never treated us special. He asked for discipline, but he didn't have to be physical to get it. And he insisted that we have a sense of direction about our roles on the ranch. We weren't just hired hands; we were part of the family.

Smokie was with the Shirleys for only a couple of years. After he graduated from high school he moved on, but for the time we were there, we both felt safe. We felt as if there was a chance we were going to grow old, maybe even get to be normal kids. Smokie was a bit of an introvert then, very much to himself, very quiet, and he still is. I was, too, for a while, but once I got a little confidence, I became more social and learned how to adapt around people.

Once Smokie and I started living with the Shirleys, we were able to do all the things we never got to do before. Our dad was so worried about us getting hurt in sports and ruining our rope-trick careers, he wouldn't let us do anything. Now we finally got to play basketball and compete in track. Both Smokie and I were pretty good in sports, but then there were only forty kids in the whole school, so being pretty good wasn't all that tough.

I went from having grades in the C's, D's, and F's to pretty much straight A's. I got a few B's, but I was on the honor roll almost every quarter I was in high school. Smokie became a good student, too. Schoolwork came a little harder for him, but he studied harder than I did. That seems to be the way with a lot of siblings. One will be a good student and things will come easy, and the other will be a good student because he worked hard at it. I probably could have gotten all A's if I'd studied, but all I wanted to do was play basketball, run on the track team, and chase girls.

This was in the mid-1970s, and all the other kids were listening to rock and roll. I didn't. I listened to country music, and I dressed like a cowboy. I didn't do a lot of the things the other kids were doing. I was too grown up for some of it, and I'd seen some things in life that a lot of those kids would never see. But I was still popular. I was the student body president, and I was on the varsity basketball team, so I wasn't a total square. In a small school like that, even if you were a little bit square, you could still be part of the "in" crowd.

As far as girlfriends went, I had a few of them, too. You had to be careful not to trade around too often because you didn't have to be very outgoing before you'd gone through every eligible girl around. Changing girlfriends was hard in another way, too, because we all knew each other so well that the girls were more like our sisters than girlfriends.

Smokie was never too interested in riding horses. He was more interested in the machinery, and putting up hay, and being more mechanical. It's what led him into the Coast Guard right out of high school. After he left the ranch, he kept up his rope tricks a little bit. He can still do a few, and he rides once in a while, but he never really got into being a horseman and a cowboy like I did. It seems that if you grow up on a ranch, you either leave hoping you never see a cow or a horse again, or you spend the rest of your life trying to figure out how to get a ranch of your own put together. It seems to be one extreme or the other.

Smokie has a wife and kids now, and he has a happy life. We see each other every so often, but I don't feel as if we have to reaffirm our relationship because we've been through so much together. I guess it must be like having gone to war with someone. Side by side, we felt fear and we shared it, and we held each other when we were scared that we were both going to die. Living through the tough times together created a bond that is everlasting. If I've needed him, he's been there for me. When my first wife, Adrian, was in a coma, he left his Coast Guard station and took the chance of getting in quite a bit of trouble with his superiors, because he had to be with his little brother at such an awfully desperate time.

Smokie is a great guy. We will always be the best of friends, and we will always love each other deeply.

Forrest told me one time, "Son, if you want to ensure that you'll always be able to eat, learn how to ride a colt and learn how to shoe a horse." He taught me how to shoe horses, and, believe me, it wasn't pretty. The only horses that neighboring ranchers trusted me with were the ones that were about as tough to shoe as anything that came down the line. They figured there wasn't a lot of risk in letting me try to tack a set of shoes on them.

It didn't take me too long to figure out that I wanted to make my living with my head higher than my butt, so I learned how to ride colts. Forrest raised a lot of Appaloosas and some Quarter Horses on the ranch, and he got me started riding the youngsters. It was pretty rough, and some of the things we did weren't very kind, but we did the best we could with what we knew. We'd tie up a hind foot to get the young horse saddled. Then I'd step on while Forrest threw the gate open, and off I'd go for a ride. It was a rough deal. We didn't work horses in a round corral, and it never dawned on us that getting a horse comfortable might help us live a little longer.

Most days were very long ones. These horses weren't Ladybirds. I wasn't being put on pets. There were a lot of wrecks, a lot of bronc rides, and a lot of runaways. In those days, everything we did seemed to be in a big cloud of dust. I rode a lot of tough horses at the ranch, and I learned what the reality of riding is all about.

I rode colts all through my junior and senior years of high school. I'd get up at four-thirty in the morning and ride two or three young ones before I'd get on the bus to go to school. In the evening, I'd ride another one or two when the weather allowed. That gave me quite a bit of experience by the time I turned eighteen, and I'd made a little money at it. For each kid Forrest and Betsy took in, the county gave them only a hundred bucks a month, so we foster kids had to help pay for our meals, clothes, and other expenses. By riding other people's colts, I made enough to pay my share. I even saved enough to buy a used tan-and-rust four-door Plymouth Belvedere sedan that had more rust than paint. Smokie and I drove it back and forth to basketball practice when school was in session.

Anytime we could spring out of the ranch was a big party for us, and we'd take off and go to a rodeo. None of us could afford a horse trailer or roping horses, so we'd throw a bronc saddle in the trunk of our car and take off for the weekend. Saddle broncs were my event. We didn't have much money, but we could live pretty cheap, and like a lot of kids in those days, we'd figure out a way to get someone to buy us a couple of bottles of Boone's Farm or Annie Green Springs. If not, we'd forgo eating so we could afford a couple of bottles of that two-dollar wine.

And away we'd go riding bucking horses, chewing tobacco, telling cowboy stories, and chasing girls—all the stuff kids do that we hope to hell our own kids don't do. We never hurt anybody, and it was a pretty harmless kind of fun.

I looked up to Royce because I thought he was pretty cool. He was older than I was, and he was a cowboy, which is what I wanted to be. I tried to copy some of things that he did, like chew tobacco. All the other cowboys that I was hanging around chewed, and I guess that's why I started. I quit a number of years ago, and I'm just glad I never got into doing drugs, or anything like that, because quitting chew was hard enough to do.

I didn't ride many broncs during my senior year in high school. In fact, I had pretty much quit rodeoing. It seemed every time I'd go, it was a net loss. Even if I rode well and made a little money, by the time I'd finished driving my car here and there across the country, buying meals and chasing around with the girls, I didn't have anything left.

I enjoyed riding bucking horses. I wasn't bad at it, and I rode a few, but it didn't take me too long to figure out I had a lot better future learning how to get them to quit bucking. I was going to need a little nest egg to get out on my own, so after I graduated, I stayed home and rode colts all summer.

I've long since gotten over the hard times that I had as a kid, and I've learned from the things that pointed me toward the future rather than kept me in the past. Sometimes people may not understand how to approach an abused horse or one that's had a lot of trouble. They're so afraid of making mistakes that sometimes the biggest mistake they make is doing nothing. If the Shirleys had dwelled on the troubles my brother and I had had instead of providing us with discipline and a sense of direction, we would eventually have become spoiled, even more spoiled than kids who had been raised in a privileged home with unlimited amounts of money and material possessions. We'd have been spoiled because we'd have realized that Forrest and Betsy were willing to make exceptions for us because of our situation. Thank goodness they didn't do that.

That time in my life, from the first day on the Shirleys' ranch, made me understand the needs of horses that have been treated poorly and are scared or troubled. You can't just fix things by showing them love while doing nothing with them. You have to give them some direction, a purpose, a job. They need something to do, a direction to take, a vision of the future so that the past eventually becomes irrelevant. A mistreated horse has more needs than a horse that has had a nice upbringing. You need to be understanding, and you need to have empathy, but you also need to know that an excess of empathy can get you into trouble. You need to provide discipline without forcing it.

Discipline isn't a dirty word. Far from it. Discipline is the one thing that separates us from chaos and anarchy. Discipline implies timing. It's the precursor to good behavior, and it never comes from bad behavior. People who associate discipline with punishment are wrong: with discipline, punishment is unnecessary.

Without discipline, it would be easy to become the kind of man my dad was.

Generally speaking, I despise and loathe noxious weeds. Some would think this is because they're the scourge of the West, and because they deprive the cattle on our ranch from eating perfectly good grass that would otherwise have grown there. Actually, there are many scourges of the West, and although noxious weeds are one, I have other reasons for not liking them.

Starting about the time I was thirteen, I began to develop an imagination that was a little too busy for the adults around me to manage. Out back of our log horse barn was a small pasture that sat right on the creek bottom. It was a nice shady spot, and it was the home of our milk cow. She was a Jersey, a credit to her breed and gender, except that she was world famous among our cowboys who hated milking because she had terribly small teats.

Her pasture wasn't used for anything else because it was completely full of cockleburs. Some refer to these botanical wonders as "burdock." It'll grow six feet high, and some plants have hundreds of burrs on them. If you get them in your hair, you just about have to get a haircut. Those burrs are like balls of Velcro or something out of a science-fiction movie.

Every once in a while, between calving and putting up hay and winter feeding, we'd have a little time on our hands in between projects on the ranch. That's when occasionally I'd find myself bordering on getting into trouble. Forrest was always quite cognizant of this. He knew what I had in mind way before I'd even thought about it. About the time I was going to start causing trouble with the other boys or was on the verge of destroying something, I'd find myself down in the milk-cow pasture chopping weeds with a shovel. Forrest would send me down there with nothing but an irrigating shovel and instructions to dig up the burdock.

This task was tough when properly equipped for the battle, but armed with only a dull irrigating shovel, it was a mammoth undertaking for a little whelp like me. I hated that job. Every thirty days or so, I'd find myself back down in the pasture where it seemed there were three times as many cockleburs as there had been before—all that chopping had merely made them spread out.

For a few years I didn't really catch on to the relationship between mischievous behavior and weed cutting. As I got a little older, I began to behave a little better. A certain sense of maturity came on, I guess. I was making money on my own then, riding colts and becoming more responsible, and I didn't have to chop cockleburs quite as often.

However, about the time I was a senior in high school, I found myself down in the cow pasture again. I don't remember exactly what I had done wrong, but it probably had something to do with staying out too late. I wasn't too far from striking out and living on my own, and I figured I knew damn near everything a fellow needed to know.

Loaded with this infinite wisdom, I finally went up to the house and said, "Forrest, I've decided that you don't have a very good system here. You don't really know much about weeds, because I've been cutting weeds for five years on this ranch, and they're just as bad now as they ever were, if not worse. And I've chopped my last weed. I refuse to cut another cocklebur. If you'll go get a weed sprayer, I'll be happy to spray every weed on the ranch, but cutting weeds is the dumbest thing I've ever heard of."

He just laughed. He never said a thing—he just laughed.

A few months later I moved out on my own and started pursuing my life. Oddly enough, within two weeks after I left, Forrest went to town and bought a weed sprayer. It took one trip through to kill every cocklebur in the cow pasture. And they never came back.

Of course, at the time, I thought Forrest was trying to get me to kill all the weeds. He was actually having me preserve them until he was done raising his boys, and I was the last one. After I was gone he didn't need the burdock anymore. The weed patch had served its purpose.

Sometimes you'll work with colts that may be a little bit the way I was, kind of looking for an adventure when time permits. These colts are not bad, they don't want to be bad, and they're not trying to make things bad for you. They just might need a little something to do. They don't need to be whipped, or knocked on, any more than I did as a kid. They just need to be directed, or better yet, redirected. So the work you do with colts like this may be like putting them in the cocklebur patch for a period of time. But don't make them spend all their time in there. Give them opportunities to come out. You'll find that eventually they'll catch on. Punishing a horse for doing something wrong is no solution. A kick in the gut solves nothing. You'll be farther ahead of the game if you redirect him toward where you'd like him to go.

Whenever I think back to the cocklebur patch, I realize we all have our weeds to clear in life. I learned more with that shovel than I can say. At the time, I sure wished Forrest had bought that weed sprayer a lot earlier, but he didn't, and he probably saved me from the "domino effect" of bad behavior had my idle time gone unchecked.

This was the first example in my life of a person making the wrong thing difficult, and the right thing easy, as opposed to making the wrong thing impossible through intimidation. Forrest and Betsy gave me an understanding of what real love was about, what devotion meant, and how a lesson can be shared, not dictated. I think, above all, Forrest gave me a clear understanding of the difference between discipline and punishment.

3
On My Own

WHEN I GOT OUT of high school, I went to work for a ranch near Harrison, Montana, a cow/calf outfit that produced about five hundred calves a year. I spent the better part of that first summer building and patching fences and irrigating.

The rancher wasn't as interested in riding as he was in farming, but he did have two colts, and he asked me to start them for him. It was just what I wanted to do, so in my mind two seemed like two hundred. Otherwise, it wasn't much of a job, but I needed it badly.

I hadn't had much formal training working with young horses back then. The day I started, I got one of the colts saddled up, led him into the corral, and just tied him to the fence. Now, when a colt wants to buck, you can see it coming, and this little guy really wanted to buck. I thought, Well, I'll just get on and off him a few times while I've got him tied to the fence, so at least I've got a fair chance when I turn him loose.

And that's when things fell apart. The moment I got on the colt, he pulled back and bucked forward. We had a hell of a time, and then I'd peel myself off. After a little bit of this, I was sitting there thinking things were going pretty well. I was enjoying the elevated view when the colt pulled back again and broke the halter rope six inches from the halter.

If that happened to me today, I would be in a six-foot-tall round corral, from which it would be hard for a horse to escape. On that day, however, the only thing I had surrounding me was a hog-wire fence about four feet high. The ranch didn't have a round corral or an arena or anything like it, just a hog pen.

There are moments in life where certain odd thoughts go through your mind, and this was one of them. The sun wasn't quite up yet, but that sky was a bright blue. I remember thinking how pretty it was. Then, after a nanosecond of stillness, off went the colt bucking and kicking with me pulling leather for everything I was worth.

The colt jumped the hog-pen fence and bucked out into the adjoining pasture. He'd run and buck, and there wasn't a thing I could do but just try to stay on him. I knew if I tried to get off at this point, I was going to get hurt.

I don't know how long I was out there. It was my first time ever riding a horse without reins, and it seemed as if it went on for hours. He'd stop and stand frozen, and every time I'd try to get him to move he'd go to bucking again. We were maybe a mile and a half from the house by the time I got him to move without bucking, but I couldn't direct him because I didn't have a halter rope to work with, so I just kept him moving.

In my wisdom of all of eighteen years, I figured that eventually the colt would want to go home. I kept working him with leg pressure and eventually we ended up back at the barn. My dismount was more like a bailout, but we made it back in one piece.

I'd like to think that skill has prevented me from getting hurt many times in my life, but luck doesn't hurt either.

An important ranch chore is putting up hay. That means you cut it, ready it to be baled, and then you stack the bales. Real summer fun in cow country.

One day I was driving a swather, a machine for mowing hay. All I'd ever wanted to be was a cowboy, so I didn't really want to be driving machinery and putting up hay. Still, when the boss pointed out a field and said, "Mow it," that's what I did.

The swather unit was not in the best shape. The drivers, which are similar to a car's transmission, slipped. You could run it on level ground, but the problem became amplified when you had to work a hill, of which the ranch had many.

I got up on top of one of the hills, but I hadn't been informed that it was a piece of hay meadow that was never cut. That's because it was too steep; the bottom of the hill dropped off about six feet and into a swamp.

My heart started pounding pretty hard when I saw the lay of the terrain in front of me. I was a little afraid of the machinery, but I figured my boss knew what he'd gotten me into, so I tipped the swather off over the hill.

What followed was another one of those moments where time stands still. After a brief moment of peace with the cornflower blue sky above, off I went downhill, going faster by the moment.

I did what I might have done with a runaway colt: I tried to pull his head around. I pulled back on one of the control levers real hard, which resulted in what looked like one of those Saturday-morning cartoon wrecks. I had stacked this machine up in the middle of a wheel-line irrigation system. Everything was wrecked: the irrigation system and the swather. It was a mess.

I got out of the swather and stood there reviewing the results of my labor for the morning. A momentary quiet graced the earth, and all was at peace. Then I started walking back toward the ranch headquarters.

As I walked by the shop, the boss asked where I was going.

"Going to the house," I said, still walking.

He asked what had happened.

"Well, we had a little accident."

He looked at me for a minute and asked, "What did you do?"

I looked at the ground for another minute, and replied, "Well, just had a little wreck."

His expression changed. "Where's the swather?"

"It's in the field," I said.

"What did you do?" He was starting to get a little touchy now.

I paused a minute and looked him square in the eye. "I wrecked it."

He kind of slumped as he realized what was next, and said, "Well, you can just go to the house, and you can pack your—"

"I'm already there," I said.

I was fired, and I can't blame him. I was costing him a lot of money, ruining his equipment. But maybe if I hadn't been fired, I might have quit, anyway. For some reason I'd known that that was kind of the end of the deal.

Besides, it was the end of the summer, and the work was about over. I'd been talking to an outfit over by Three Forks, Montana. It was called the Madison River Cattle Company, and it had a lot of cattle and it raised horses. It was my kind of place. I was definitely on my way to becoming a cowboy.

When I went to meet with the ranch manager and talk about a job, he was in town at a Ray Hunt clinic. A teacher in high school had told me about Hunt and the wonderful things he could do with a horse. I thought that was just a made-up story and said, "Ah, he doesn't have anything he can teach me."

The teacher had replied, "If you ever want to see how the pros do it, you need to look him up." Mrs. Jackson wasn't going to argue with me. I was about at the age where I knew everything about everything, and the teacher was smart enough to know there wasn't any point in saying any more.

I headed into town to visit with the manager and see just what this Ray Hunt clinic was all about. I arrived at the arena and took a seat at the top of the grandstand, but there wasn't much going on. It was lunchtime, and I couldn't find the ranch manager.

I was getting up to leave when into the arena came Ray Hunt and Tom Dorrance, another legendary horseman. They started working with their horses, and all of a sudden I noticed some things that Ray Hunt's saddle horse was doing that I didn't know a horse could do, moving from side to side and bending and backing with no visible effort from the rider.

I moved down closer to the action, and closer again until I was standing right by the round corral. I peeked through the rails and watched Ray's every move. I just couldn't believe it. I never knew a horseman could be that good. And, of course, Tom Dorrance was there helping Ray in the clinic and also doing some things that I thought were just magical.

Ray started working with a young broncy horse that wanted to strike out. In my experience you saddled such a horse by tying up a hind leg to immobilize him so you could get the saddle on him. But Ray worked the colt at the end of a rope, moving the colt's hindquarters right and left and the forequarters right and left, basically teaching the horse to dance. Ray already knew the theory behind the dance:

when you control a horse's feet, you also can control that the horse doesn't move unless and until you ask him to.

By the time Ray had that colt saddled, I said to myself, "There's *really* something going on there." I knew I'd have had a hard time saddling that colt, and I was a good hand with horses.

That was the first time I ever saw a person work a horse that way, using his understanding of a horse's mind and body to train with kindness and to end up getting some of the sharpest turns and hardest stops I'd ever seen. And all with a plain snaffle bit. What's more, the horse looked happy, as if he enjoyed being with the man. His expression showed contentment in his eyes.

Seeing Ray Hunt in action was just a brief encounter, but it impressed me no end.

The ranch manager saw me and came over. "I guess you want to talk about that cowboying job on the ranch?" he said.

"Sir, I would," I told him. "But if you'd excuse me, I'm trying to watch this gentleman work horses. So if it's okay with you, we're going to have to talk a little later."

Well, that kind of took him aback some. We didn't really visit that afternoon, but we had other chances because I returned for the rest of the Ray Hunt clinic. I was hooked for life. To this day I'm still trying to pursue the magic that I saw that man do.

I got the job at the Madison River Cattle Company. The manager took quite an interest in me and started sending me to Ray Hunt clinics. Ray Hunt gives the initial impression of being the most secure, unaffected person you'd ever meet. The things he taught me about horses and the things he's taught me about myself have changed my life. The approach that he has to working with horses was like nothing I'd ever seen, nor probably ever will see again. He's a great horseman, and a fine gentleman. I admired him so much that I wanted nothing more than to be just like him. He and his wife, Carolyn, have been like parents to me. They have treated me like family through the years, and for that I'll forever be indebted to them.

When I showed up at the ranch a few days after the clinic, the cow boss, Mel, showed me the bunkhouse and the cookhouse. When we sat down for dinner, he said, "We're going to be gathering cattle tomorrow. If you like, you might want to catch that roan horse out there. That's going to be one of your horses; the whole pen of horses is going to be your string. Some of the other boys have had a little trouble with them, but you shouldn't have any problem, although you might want to ride him around the corral and get some of the kinks out of him before we go gather. It's pretty rough country."

I thought, Sure, no problem.

So after dinner, I went out and ran the little roan horse into the round corral. I had to rope him as he was a little broncy, but I thought, Well, no big deal. I got him saddled up with no trouble. I didn't know anything about groundwork or getting a horse loosened up or relaxed. I thought I'd just step up on him.

Well, that horse bucked so hard, he bucked my hat clear out of the corral. I stayed on him, but by the time he was finished bucking, I felt as if I'd experienced a seizure. "What have I gotten myself into?" I asked myself when I stopped shaking.

The next morning we saddled the horses in the barn, then hauled them about thirty miles in a truck and trailer up into the hills where the cattle were. After we arrived, Mel said, "Here, let me help you get that roan horse ready."

Back in those days Mel knew just enough about Ray Hunt's techniques to be dangerous. He was working the horse on the end of the halter rope from his saddle horse, and he told me, "Go ahead, Buck, get on. I've got you snubbed up"—snubbed up meaning he had a hold of the horse—"so you won't have any problem with him bucking. I'll just dally up, and it'll shut him down." That meant he would wrap the rope around his saddle horn; the confinement would keep the roan under control.

Not quite. As soon as I climbed on, Roany started bucking. It seemed as if he bucked in four directions at the same time. Every time I'd just about get in sync with his bucking in a straight line, Mel would ride off and jerk his head around. That sent him off in another direction, which made it ten times harder to ride. I'd have been better off if Roany had broken the halter and gotten away. Then at least he'd have bucked in a straight line.

I was a dishrag when Roany decided to quit bucking. Mel took off at a trot on a long uphill grade. I had enough experience to know that if I was going to survive the day, I needed to get Roany out of breath. We trotted what seemed like six miles up the grade until we got to the top, but Roany hadn't even broken a sweat.

Mel halted and let his horse rest. He was looking for cattle through his binoculars and having a nice break. I was getting a little nervous with Roany standing around catching his own breath, and I thought, Come on, Mel, let's keep moving.

On a normal day you might think, Ah, the sweet smell of sage on a frosty clear morning. Wrong-o. All I could smell was nervous sweat. And as Roany's respiration began to slow, mine sped up in anticipation of the next move in our dance together. Mel kept looking and looking. Because I was new on the job, I didn't want to say, "Mel, I need to get the hell out of here and get going." I was sitting very still, trying to convince Roany that nobody was on his back.

Finally, about the time Mel was ready to go, Roany took a big old deep breath. His respiration returned to normal. His batteries were recharged. We tipped off the hill and hadn't gone two steps before Roany started bucking. And I mean bucking. The hill was steep enough so that he was clearing about fifty feet at a jump. As Mel cheered me on, Roany and I bucked all the way to the bottom.

I learned my lesson about the dangers of standing still, of not having my horse's legs under my control. For the rest of the day, we stayed at a high trot, and I survived it, even with Roany bucking all day long.

Roany was quite a project for me. The first hundred days I rode him, he bucked every single day. After a few months, however, I wised up and started spending some time around

Ray Hunt. Thanks to the techniques I learned about hooking on and getting a horse to move his feet, Roany gradually improved. I finally got him to the point that I could swing a rope on him and get some ranch work done.

One day we were up in that same country where we'd been gathering cattle that first day. Roany had stopped bucking and was serious about his work, but being a kid, I couldn't leave well enough alone.

I was bored because there weren't any cattle to rope at the moment. I wanted to rope something, so I roped a little tiny sagebrush about the size of a small potted plant. I dallied off and pulled it up out of the ground. Little did I realize that this tiny piece of sagebrush had roots about thirty feet long. I pulled and I pulled, and the rope was stretched to twice its length when that little piece of sagebrush finally came loose and flew right up under Roany's tail.

Roany clamped his tail down so tight that you couldn't have pulled that sagebrush out with a pickup truck. And off he went. He didn't buck me off, but he used me plumb up. Plus that little stunt of mine probably set me back a few weeks in his training. I had been really getting somewhere, and then I pulled a trick like that. I learned another valuable lesson that day, that time about me.

The day came when Roany was sold. I knew it was coming. We raised horses to sell, but Roany and I had been through a lot together, and it was a sad day for me. All I could think about were the times on the way to the barn that I'd say, "God, give me one more ride with Roany. Just don't let him kill me today." The next day I'd say, "God, I know I said I wouldn't ask for anything else yesterday, but it's me again." Then we got to be partners, and pulling my saddle off him in the sales ring made me sad to see him go out the door and off to a new life with a new owner.

An old man who lived near Deer Lodge, Montana, bought Roany. He roped steers on him and used him on the ranch the rest of his life. They got along great. Roany had a good home, and I'm glad because he was an important milestone in my career: he was the one I was going through hell with about the time I first was exposed to the kind of riding I do today.

Another memorable lesson during my time at the Madison River Cattle Company came when I was working with a very troubled horse named Ayatollah. Needless to say, like his namesake, he was a bit of a terrorist: we'd been through quite a few bronco rides. Ayatollah would buck you off if you cleared your throat, so you didn't have to do very much to get yourself into trouble.

I'd been trying to get him to do a turnaround, a move where the horse brings his front feet across while pivoting on a hind foot. It's a quick and efficient way to move away from something fearful and a very natural movement for a horse in the wild, but encouraging a horse to turn around while you're sitting on his back can be a bit tricky.

One day, I was watching Ray Hunt do a demonstration at the indoor arena at Montana State University. A couple of guys had brought him a colt that was kind of a setup; they wanted to make Ray look bad because he was pretty controversial in those days. People thought that the notion of getting along with a horse, communicating with the horse, and even, God forbid, being friends with a horse was forsaking the western image of being a cowboy.

Out came the horse, a five-year-old black stud colt. Both ears were frozen off, and his mane and tail were full of burrs. A real pitiful-looking animal, and touchy, too. The two old boys herded their horse into a round corral that had been set up in an indoor arena, then they waited with smirks on their faces. They just knew they were going to get that old man—Ray was in his fifties—in a wreck.

Ray knew he was being set up, so he told the owners, "I can see you take a lot of pride in your horses. I know you have a bright future for this colt, so I guess I'd better get him leading." Ray, who had been born with a clubfoot, kind of limped into the corral. A few minutes inside, and he could tell he wouldn't be safe on foot, so got up on a saddle horse.

Using patience and skill, in under ten minutes Ray had the colt leading and standing right beside the saddle horse so Ray could rub him with his rope's coils.

Within another five minutes, Ray had the colt saddled. But when he turned the colt loose, everything came undone. The colt bucked and kicked, the stirrups hitting on his back at every jump.

Ray, who was then on foot in the corral, kept the colt moving around. He thréw a rope around the colt's neck, then led the horse up to him and petted him down the forehead. Turning to the owners, he said, "I don't want to hold up you boys' progress, so I'd just better ride him."

By now these guys were thinking that maybe they'd set up the wrong man, but they were still fairly confident because Ray still had to get the colt ridden.

The colt had the rope around his neck. Ray looped a part of the rope across the colt's nose to get him bending toward him, pulled down the stampede string of his hat and tucked it under his chin, and stepped onto the colt.

Ray was wearing a down coat, the kind that makes more noise than you'd want to be making on a young sensitive colt. He unzipped the coat and slipped out of it. With his rope in one hand and the coat in the other, Ray reached back and tapped the colt on both hips.

Everyone watching waited for the explosion, but the colt just loped off like the gentlest son-of-a-buck you ever threw a leg over.

Ray allowed the horse to stop, and then said to the men, "Well, considering how far you boys plan to take your colt, I'm sure you'd like him to turn around a bit." With that, Ray reached forward with his coat, and the horse turned.

Turned? The colt spun so fast he was a blur. I don't know how Ray's hat stayed on his head, even with the stampede string under his chin.

Ray then shook the rope in his other hand, and the colt spun the other way. With that, Ray loped the horse around the corral, through the gate, and continued to lope around the indoor arena. While he was at it, he asked the colt to make three or four lead changes. The colt obliged, and with beautiful clean changes, too.

Then Ray galloped the colt down to where its owners were standing—and I mean *galloped*—ending with the most beautiful sliding stop you ever saw.

Ray flipped the loop of the rope over the colt's nose, stepped down, and offered the rope to the men. "Well, boys, I guess I got him ready for you," he said.

One of the guys started to reach out, then pulled his hand back as if from a hot branding iron. "No, Ray," he said, "I think the horse has had enough for the day."

Ray looked the guys in the eye and replied, "Well, boys, I don't know whether you got what you came for, but this horse did."

I couldn't wait to try this new way of turning out on Ayatollah. When I got home, I hung my coat on top of the round pen fence where I could reach it from horseback. Then I caught Ayatollah.

When I got him saddled, he was walking-on-eggs edgy. As we tiptoed around the corral, I got closer and closer to my coat, and when I was close enough I grabbed it. He didn't explode, but that hump in his back was so big it looked as if I had left my lunch under the saddle blanket.

Finally, the time came for me to work on the turnaround. I stuck my coat in Ayatollah's face, and he turned so fast everything was just a blur. I didn't realize the centrifugal force of a turning horse could be that strong. I was losing count of the turns he made when suddenly I was flying off the front of him. I'd have hit the ground if my left spur hadn't hung up on the back of my saddle.

I found myself looking right into his eyes, and he was as terrified as I was. Dropping the coat never crossed my mind; absolute terror had taken over my entire body, and my hands were paralyzed into clenched fists. The longer I held the coat out there, the harder he spun.

Ayatollah was spinning and spinning and spinning, and he wouldn't stop. Although I knew full well that if I could somehow get off him that he would probably kick me before I hit the ground, I decided to do what I could to free my spur from the cantle and take my chances.

When I finally kicked loose, Ayatollah drove my head into the ground at what felt like a hundred miles an hour. My lower jaw plowed up maybe two pounds of dirt and manure. What I didn't plow up with my lower jaw, I scooped up with my belt buckle, so the rest of that dirt and manure went down my pants.

Just as I slammed into the ground like a lawn dart, Ayatollah did indeed kick out at me. His right hind foot landed on my right ear. He didn't kick me in the head, but my ear swelled up about as big as a mitten.

As I lay on the ground with Ayatollah bucking around the corral, I remembered one small detail (evidently that bump on my head jogged loose a little memory I should have drawn on prior to getting on Ayatollah): when Ray Hunt did the spins, he reached back with the hand that didn't have a coat in it and held on to the Cheyenne roll on the cantle of his saddle. That kept him from going over the front of his horse when he started to turn.

That was quite an important point, and I learned it well. The next time I attempted to turn Ayatollah with my coat, I gave him a very measured, very small, portion of coat, and I gave myself a very large portion of Cheyenne roll to cling to with my free hand. The turns worked out a lot better, and since then I've never had to remind myself about preparing for the consequences of a fast turn.

That lesson was better than any clinic I could have gone to.

After I left the Madison River Cattle Company in 1982, I went to work for a horse outfit near Bozeman. I had been doing things my teachers had shown me, but I'd also seen that this gentle approach to working horses still had quite a bit of opposition. People were real apt to hang on to their old ways and not try anything new. These days, what I do with horses is very popular, but it sure wasn't back then.

I was taking morning classes at Montana State University in Bozeman and then going back to the outfit to ride colts in the afternoon. I didn't ride the owner's colts, though. He had hired other trainers for them, and those guys had their own ideas.

In the barn one day after class, I saw the owner and one of his trainers trying to halterbreak a filly. They had led the filly and her mare into a stall, jammed the filly into a corner, and muscled the halter over her head any way they could. Then they led the mare out toward a fence, and when the filly followed, they tied her to a post and led the mare away.

You can imagine the wreck that resulted. The little filly had absolutely no preparation for standing, so naturally she pulled back and fought. She struck out with her feet, and she flipped over. By the time I arrived, she had been upside down who knows how many times. Now two grown men were stomping on her head, kicking her in the belly, and beating her with the metal bull snaps on their halter ropes. When that didn't work, one of them poured a bucket of water into her ears to try to get her to stand up. The filly did get up, but then she'd fight again and fall back down.

The filly was insane with fear. She jumped up, but as soon as she felt that tight halter rope, she flipped over again and got hung upside down by her head. If you've ever heard young horses in agony make a certain pitiful, desperate sound just before they die, that's the sound she was making. I shuddered to imagine what it was like for her mother to hear that from a distance and not be able to do a thing about it.

The next thing I knew, these two brain surgeons were dragging a hose toward her. They were going to douse her real hard to try to get her up and then keep her on her feet.

I had stayed out of their way until now. They had mocked my way of working with horses. Even though I had more than once bailed them out by helping them with trailer loading, they had dismissed everything I had done for them. But when I saw they were planning to hose water down the filly's ears, I couldn't stand it any longer. I unsnapped the lead rope so the filly could get her head down, then I snapped another lead shank to the halter.

It didn't take me more than a few seconds of gentle persuasion to get her up. I rubbed on her forehead for a moment or two, and in less than five minutes I had her leading all over the arena.

These two supposed horse trainers should have been embarrassed or ashamed, but they were so overcome with anger, they weren't able or chose not to see what they had done to this little filly. And they were upset that I had succeeded.

I led the filly back to one of the men, the one who owned the operation, and handed him the lead rope. I looked him right in the eye and didn't say a word. I didn't have to. He saw my anger and resentment.

I rolled up my bed, and when he woke up the next morning, I was long gone. There was no way I was going to change him, and I certainly wasn't going to be around that kind of behavior. I moved to Gallatin Gateway, to another indoor arena up the Gallatin Canyon at Spanish Creek.

While I was making a living riding colts, I was also pursuing my roping. After Smokie and I had moved in with the

Shirleys, our trick-roping careers had ground to a halt. Betsy and Forrest knew nothing about the rodeo business, especially how to promote us as Dad had done. In my junior year in high school, one of my teachers asked me to play Santa Claus and do rope tricks in the Christmas play. I hadn't spun a rope in a while, at least not in a show, but I said I would and started to practice. Everybody in the little town of Harrison was in the school gym that evening, and when I finished, I got a standing ovation.

I kept on practicing a minimum of three hours a day, seven days a week, even long after I got out of high school. Three years later, after I was reinstated in the Professional Rodeo Cowboys Association (my membership had lapsed), I got good enough at the Texas Skip to set a world record by hopping in and out of the loop 980 jumps in a row. This record was later shattered by my friend Vince Bruce, an Englishman who did something like two or three thousand jumps.

Thanks to the Santa Claus skit, the show-business bug had taken ahold, and just about the time I got back into the PRCA, I became involved with the State Department's Friendship Force. That led to travel as a part-time goodwill ambassador helping promote U.S. tourism. My first trip was to Japan as part of a group that included a number of Native American dancers, some country-and-western musicians, and the 1980 Miss Montana, Wendy Holton. The Japanese loved cowboys, and there I was, eighteen years old, now over six feet tall, with blond hair, surrounded by beautiful Japanese girls, and keeping company with Miss

Buck on an international tour with the Friendship Force, spinning ropes for the local media in Newcastle, England.

Montana. I was about as close to being John Wayne as I was ever going to get, and when the tour was over, I really didn't want to leave.

My stint with the Friendship Force convinced me there was no reason I couldn't make a good living doing rope tricks. I put what money I had together and took off for Denver and the big stock show held there every year.

The rodeo producers held a convention at the Brown Palace Hotel, where you went to get your jobs for the year. You promoted yourself by renting a booth and putting up a little display. Because my dad had always handled that part of the business, I knew very little about it. I hadn't realized

Buck in Costa Rica with Mike Thomas, manager of the Madison River Cattle Company.

there was a lot more needed than just being a good trick roper, so I wasn't prepared at all.

I spent most of what little money I had on a hotel room, and most of the rest for booth space, but I had nothing to put on the booth. A friend named Doug Deter helped me take some pictures out in the snow, and we put them on a poster board and tried to make some sort of a display. In addition, I had some pictures in a photo album that showed some of my rope tricks, but on the whole it was a pretty sorry presentation.

I sat for three days and watched the rodeo producers walk by and stop at the other booths. Every producer had a little contract book, and I saw contracts being signed right and left. It seemed as if everybody was signing contracts, but by the third and last day of the convention, I hadn't signed a single one. All the money I had saved up was gone, and I had no prospects. Although I was really a good trick roper, probably the best one there, no one knew.

Every day at 4:00 P.M. was happy hour, when the convention committee members passed out free booze and everybody joked, laughed, and told stories. During happy hour on the last day, a very influential rodeo producer passed my booth.

Forcing myself to summon up the courage to speak with him, I stopped him and asked, "Sir, would you take a moment and look at my album in case you would ever want someone to do some rope tricks at one of your rodeos?"

He just looked at me and said, "Son, I've looked at so goddamn many pictures today, I don't care if I look at another one."

"Well, I'm committed now," I told myself, then practically begged him to look at my pictures.

The producer didn't sit down. Instead, he just flopped my album open on a table in somebody else's booth and started flipping through the pages. He never looked at a

Buck practicing his roping around the time he was looking for rodeo work.

single one. He was laughing, joking, and greeting people across the room.

When he spilled his drink in the middle of my book, I took it away, slammed it shut, and said, "Thanks for your time."

He just glanced at me. He didn't say anything. What happened to me meant nothing to him. As you can imagine, happy hour wasn't so happy for me. I went upstairs to my room, threw down my photo album, lay on my bed, and cried. Nobody cared.

I went back to ranching and really thought about quitting rope tricks. I had a good cowboying job, but I had no roping jobs and no prospects.

Later on that summer a rodeo contractor named Roy Hunnicut out in Colorado called me. He said, "Son, I'd like to hire you to do some rope tricks for me in a few rodeos. A guy who was trick riding for me broke his leg. You're the only one who's not working. I want to give you a try at one in Rock Springs, Wyoming. If I like what you're doing, I'll give you the rest of my rodeos."

The manager of the ranch where I was working was happy for me. "As long as you come back in time to get the colts ready for the fall sale," he told me, "you go ahead and hit some of these rodeos."

I drove all night to get to Rock Springs for the Red Desert Roundup Rodeo. I didn't have much of a fancy truck, trailer, or horses. In fact, my old horse trailer featured a variety of spreading rust motifs by way of decoration. But I had some damn good rope tricks.

There were five or six thousand people in the audience. I did my best stuff, and it brought the house down. I got a standing ovation.

Since I hadn't been sure whether Hunnicut would take me on for the rest of the season, I had left some of my stuff back in Montana. A friend named Bob Donaldson had asked me to give him a ride to Douglas, Wyoming, on my way back to pick up my things. Bob, who was working the high school rodeo finals there, offered to introduce me to the producer of that event. He said, "I think he'd really like to talk to you. He's heard that your rope tricks are really good, and he really wants to give you a job. He could be a great connection for you." I knew who the man was but I didn't say a word.

When we got to Douglas early the next morning, this big-time producer was sitting around and drinking coffee with a bunch of his cronies. Bob introduced me to him, but the rodeo producer didn't recognize me. Of course he didn't; he had been too full of himself that afternoon in Denver.

He said, "Well, I'm so-and-so, and I've got a lot of big shows, some of the biggest rodeos in the business, and I heard you're really a hell of a performer. I'd like to give you some work, son."

I replied, "Well, sir, I know you don't remember me, but I certainly remember you. And it's not that I don't need the work, because I do. But working for you and going to those big rodeos wouldn't mean near as much to me as telling you to kiss my ass. You still don't remember me, and it doesn't matter. But because of what you did to me at one of the lowest points of my life, I'll never forget you. It's people like you who are going to make me successful one day."

Thanks to Roy Hunnicutt, I had plenty of success with my rope tricks, if you want to call it that. I was good at them, but it was kind of a dead-end deal. I was lucky to make $200 a performance, and by the time I'd paid my expenses, I was making less money than cowboying for $450 a month. Besides, I had a lot better time on the ranch than I did on the rodeo circuit—the loneliness of being on the road got to me, too, so after a few years, I went home to the ranch.

However, I've never forgotten the impression that "big-time" rodeo producer made on me. He wouldn't give me his time because he didn't figure I could do anything for him. He didn't respect me as a person. That was a good lesson I've never forgotten.

Always up for a good cause, Buck does the Texas Skip at a benefit for the Sheridan Inn in Sheridan, Wyoming.

Now that I've reached the point where I have a certain amount of influence, I try real hard to take time out for people who may expect not to be noticed. If somebody writes me a letter or comes up and talks to me, I appreciate the courage the effort may have taken, and I try to give them my time. I try to learn their names.

It hasn't been that long since I was in their position.

4
Learning
to Listen

BY THE EARLY 1980s I had spent a lot of time with a lot of great horsemen. I was learning how little I knew about horses and how much more I needed to learn. I'd ride horses all day and then consider the day's work while trying to sleep. I was constantly confounded, but eventually solutions would present themselves.

When I moved to Gallatin Gateway, Montana, I didn't have any customers, but I had a horse or two of my own. I rented an indoor arena up Gallatin Canyon, at the Spanish Creek Ranch, and then took an apartment in the old Gallatin Gateway Inn.

The inn, which has since been renovated, is a beautiful turn-of-the-century hotel now, but in those days it was pretty run-down. The owner had been trying to remodel the place, and like a lot of owners before him, he had run out of money. Of the two apartments next to the downstairs bar, I took the one with the broken windows because it was cheaper. It had a few carpet remnants on the floor, but it wasn't much beyond that. The bunkhouse at Madison River seemed like the Taj Mahal by comparison. The bar still had a liquor license, so a few of the local winos would come in and have a drink or two in the evenings. Otherwise, the building was vacant.

After renting the apartment and the arena, I was down to a roll of dimes, which I used to start making phone calls from the pay phone outside the bar. I called everybody I knew with a horse who might know somebody who had colts I could ride. I scored a couple, but I wasn't going to get paid until I'd ridden them and their owners were satisfied. That meant I was at least a month away from getting a paycheck.

All I had in my cupboard were a box of Krusteaz Pancake Mix and a big tub of margarine. That's pretty much what I lived on for a few weeks. And even after I was paid, there were still bills to be paid, so I continued to live on Krusteaz Pancake Mix and canned chili.

The arena at Spanish Creek was about five miles up the canyon from the inn. Times were so tough I didn't even have the money to put gas in my truck, so getting there and back meant riding a horse along the side of a fairly busy highway. In the evenings I'd trot down in the dark with the logging trucks that roared by on their way out of the mountains. I'd hobble my horse in the tall grass behind the inn and let him graze there all night. The next morning I'd get up before daylight and trot him back up to the arena. Of course, the inn's owners would have run me off if they had found out I had a horse in the backyard, but they never found out.

It was another month before I was able to put a little gas in my truck and drive back and forth.

Spanish Creek was right next door to The Flying D. I got paid to ride some of their colts, which is how I met my "partner in crime," Jeff Griffith. Jeff's dad, Bud, was the manager of The Flying D. Jeff was still living at home with his folks, and we spent quite a bit of time at Spanish Creek riding horses. During the week I helped him with some of his dad's colts, and we cowboyed together. On the weekends we'd head out to the local cowboy bars. We spent most of our money on girls and booze, and the rest of it we wasted.

In those days I was charging $125 a month to train a colt. At that rate, it worked out to close to a dollar a ride. I was still trying to get a business of my own going, and I was still practicing my rope tricks to see if I could score some TV commercials. I didn't have an agent at the time, but I was acquainted with a commercial director from Bozeman named Marcus Stevens. Marcus and I met in Gallatin Gateway and got to be friends, and he gave me quite a bit of work over the years. I also got calls from a few producers who learned about my rope tricks through the PRCA. I made commercials for, among others, Visa, Best Western Hotels, and Busch beer. The commercials took a while in coming, but once they started, they helped pay the bills.

I lived at the Gallatin Gateway Inn for a year or so; then in 1983 I moved into a trailer house on The Flying D. It wasn't much better than the room at the inn, but it was closer to my horses and saved me the drive to the arena.

After I had moved out of Forrest and Betsy's house, their son-in-law Roland, who was married to their daughter Elaine, took over the ranch. Forrest retired to Arizona, but Betsy didn't—she couldn't leave her kids and the ranch. Roland, Elaine, and Betsy stayed on the ranch many years.

Forrest died during the winter of 1984. I didn't get to go to the funeral. It was the dead of winter, and I couldn't get away; luckily I had seen him about two weeks before. I had taken a trip to Mexico with my foster brother Stuart Shirley and his wife, Annie, and we stopped over and saw Forrest for a couple of days. Forrest had just come back from the VA hospital with a clean bill of health. We had a great visit, and it never crossed anyone's mind that he wasn't going to be around much longer.

It was a real shock when Stuart called me in the middle of the night to say that Forrest had passed away. The cause was an aneurysm in his lungs. I can't describe how bad I felt. At the same time, I felt guilty. My dad was still alive at the time, and I found myself thinking I would have gladly traded my dad's life for Forrest's. I thought there must be something wrong about that, but I couldn't help feeling that way because of everything Forrest had taught me.

Solutions to problems often come from knowing when to ask for help.

While I was riding colts for the public at Spanish Creek, I was having trouble with a roan horse. I'd been working for a while on getting him to turn around and on getting him balanced. By "balanced" I mean getting him so he'd move the same way in both directions. At that point he was pretty much the same on both sides, but it was sticky going either way.

It was early morning on a fine summer day. As I looked over the top rail of the round pen, the only sound was that of my horse catching his breath. Through the steady rhythm, I realized how desperate I was to solve the problem. Nothing seemed to work. I did everything I thought was correct; for example, I tried leading with my right rein and supporting with my left rein against the base of his neck and putting my left heel against his side. Still, I didn't get any response. I couldn't get the horse to put out any effort. If I asked him to put any effort into turning to work a cow, he wouldn't go any faster. It was as if he was going in slow motion. The more I kicked and the more I pulled, the worse it got.

I was frustrated to the point of tears. I couldn't seem to make any headway.

Now, Montana may be short on population, but it fills the void with a fine lot of colloquialisms. "If you don't get it, you'd better be barking at the hole," is one of them. It means "keep trying."

I knew I needed some guidance, and since Ray Hunt was off doing a clinic and I had no way of getting ahold of him, I figured it was worth a shot to call Bill Dorrance.

Bill was Tom Dorrance's brother. He and I hadn't met yet, but for years Mike Beck, a good friend from the Madison River days, had been telling me about the man's horsemanship. They had spent quite a bit of time together on Bill's ranch near Salinas, California, and according to Mike, Bill's skill with a bridle horse and the way he handled a rope were legendary. If I was ever to be a Jedi, I needed an Obi-Wan, so I took a deep breath and called him.

"Bill, you don't know who I am," I stammered, "but I need some help with my horse. Mike Beck told me what a great horseman you are, and I've admired the things you've shown him. I hope you can help."

He didn't say anything, so I went on. "My horse turns around pretty good, but I can't seem to get him to put any effort into it." I told him all the things I had done with the horse, how frustrated I had become, and how worried I was that I was pushing this nice little horse harder than he deserved.

When Bill finally spoke, he acted as if he'd never heard a word I said. He started talking about the hindquarters. "You know, Buck, if you can move the hindquarters right or left, you can get his body arranged to where he can do some things that you didn't think he could do."

I just sat there and thought, How sad. Poor Bill has gotten so much age on him that he didn't hear what I asked him. I suppose I was hoping that Bill would tell me just to take the tail end of my McCarty rein and whack the horse across the shoulder, or maybe to turn my toe out and use my spur to move his front quarters. I had no idea why he was talking about moving the hindquarters right or left.

I asked him again, "How can I get my horse to turn around a little sharper so I can get him to work a cow a little better?"

Again he said, "You know, if a fellow can get a horse reaching backward a little bit, it will help him. It's amazing how much the hindquarters have to do with all the things you do with a horse to get a job done."

There he goes again, I told myself, he's talking about the hindquarters and avoiding my problem. It was as if he hadn't heard a word I said.

I asked Bill one more time what I should do about my problem with the front quarters because I was sure that's where the problem was. Again we ended up talking about the hindquarters. I decided that no matter how I asked him about the specifics of my problem, he wasn't able to understand me.

I decided to give up on it for that day, and we finished our conversation talking about horses we had ridden and folks we both knew. I thought we'd just had a nice conversation. At least I'd had a chance to talk to the legendary Bill Dorrance, which really meant a lot to me. So I left the other part alone.

The next day I went down to the barn to see the horse. I stood there looking into his eyes as he ate. I felt sorry for him, and I felt sorry for myself. I was feeling down on myself about the way I had been with the horse. I had been riding him really hard for a few days just to get this one fast turn out of him, and it wasn't fair of me. So I decided I would just take a ride and not fight with him. That day we would simply enjoy each other. We'd take a ride out through the hills, and I wouldn't ask him to do anything difficult or anything I didn't think we could do.

It was the fall of the year, and the leaves had started turning up in the aspens. I sensed the urgencies that seem to effect the change of seasons, and I got to thinking then about other kinds of changes, too. Perhaps this horse thing was something I wasn't going to be able to do very well. Maybe I'd rekindle my trick-roping career because I'd been pretty successful at that.

All throughout that ride I just tried to leave the horse alone, but on the way back to the barn, I stopped. The message Bill had given me kept creeping into my brain. I decided to see whether, if I could stop the horse with one rein and untrack his hindquarters a little bit, I just might get him to step over behind.

When I tried to do what Bill had so subtly suggested, my rein felt as if it was tied off to a big rock or the back of a truck going the other way. I couldn't get the horse to budge in the direction I was asking him to go. He hardly had any bend in him at all. I couldn't get him to step over with his hindquarters (move his hindquarters right or left), and that kind of surprised me.

And so I worked on getting him to step over. As down on myself as I was that day, I figured I could at least accomplish that much. At least I could get him to bend.

After much leg-pressure urging, I got the horse to untrack his hindquarters a little bit, to step over behind and bend more through his loin and rib cage. He had a little more "give" on the end of the rein, and was a little more supple in his movements. He felt lighter in my hands.

After having accomplished that little bit, I tried to keep my promise to the horse not to bother or pick on him, so I started back to the barn with a loose rein. But something continued to eat at me. I asked the horse to turn around over his hindquarters. And to my great surprise, he spun so fast that he reminded me of Ayatollah's high-velocity turns, yet he was relaxed.

I did this once, and then, remembering the other roan horse with a sagebrush stuck in his butt, I reminded myself, "You know, you better leave that horse alone because it's not going to get any better than this, that's for sure. The way you've been riding the last few days, you'll probably wreck it in the next few minutes." So I walked a brisk walk back to the barn and unsaddled the horse before I destroyed what I'd been trying to get.

While I was putting my gear away, I reviewed what had happened. There was no way I was going to get that horse to turn around any faster without freeing up his hind end. Somewhere along the line I'd lost the hindquarters. I'd had control of them at one point, but I got so busy trying to be a "horse trainer"—and I say that with much chagrin—I'd lost the basics that prepares any horse in the first place.

I also reviewed my own attitude. "I'll be damned," I told myself, "Bill tried to tell me which end of the horse needed work, but I couldn't hear it."

I called Bill again a few days later. I really wanted to tell him about my progress with the horse. We chatted about this and that, and after a few minutes, he asked, "How did things work out with that roan horse that you were telling me about?"

I said, "Well, Bill, I found that those hindquarters were not shaped up very well. His hip was in the way, it wasn't underneath him, and considering the way he was prepared, he was turning about as fast as he possibly could. I got him all shaped up now, and he's happy to turn for me. We're getting along well again."

I've often said that if you took away the fact that Bill was a great hand with a rope and a gifted horseman, what you'd have left is a really fine human being. Considering I hadn't really been listening to him the first time we talked, he could have replied in any number of ways. He might have said, "Well, I told you so," or, "If you had listened to me in the first place."

But Bill didn't. He didn't rub it in. It wasn't about being right or wrong, and he was a gentleman about it. He just said, "Well, that's real good that worked out for you, Buck. I'm

Buck working on untracking a horse's hind end. This action will ultimately help Buck to remove the "sticky" nature of the horse's hind feet and get him to move off in either direction more easily.

glad that things are starting to shape up between you and that horse." That was characteristic of Bill Dorrance's approach. He had the answer, but he never tried to ram it down my throat. That hadn't been my way: I thought I had the answer, and I had been trying to ram it down the horse's throat.

That first phone call to Bill changed my life, and for the better. But although I was thrilled with the discovery that would help horses in the future, I was depressed by my own stupidity and all the horses that I could have helped. I was mad at myself, and it was many days before I got over it.

Years later I was doing some ranch-roping clinics, showing people how to handle their horses and catch and work with cattle in a nonabusive way. Many of the people at one clinic in Watsonville, California, were real green, so I had to do all of the roping myself. I'd rope the cattle around the neck and get them gentled, and the people would ride up and throw heel shots. Of course, a lot of their horses had never seen a cow before; they had been raised in backyards, and as far as they knew, a horse was lunch for a cow.

I had no idea Bill was there. He had gotten a ride down from his ranch with one of my cowboy friends, and he was part of the audience watching the clinic.

I usually have a pretty good eye for picking a gentle cow to rope. I picked one out, but I made a bad shot or two, and I missed. It was pretty easy roping, and I shouldn't have missed, but nevertheless I did. I finally got a good shot off, but it landed on the wrong animal. Instead of that gentle steer, I roped a wild steer. Right off he wanted to fight, and run up my rope and hook my horse. I wished there had been a good roper in the bunch of riders in the arena with me: I wanted somebody who could slip in and throw a heel shot, pick up the hind feet, and get that steer down on the ground so I could get my rope back, then pretend it never happened and go pick on something else.

But there wasn't anybody like that in this group, and I couldn't get my rope back. I fought with the steer, and he jumped around and bawled and was mad as hell. I finally got him slowed down, but things were supposed to have gone smooth. That's what my clinics are supposed to be all about, and this was anything but smooth.

As if that weren't bad enough, it was the first time Bill Dorrance had ever seen me do a ranch-roping clinic, the first time he'd seen me roping on cattle, and I had missed a couple of easy shots.

We had dinner together that night, and I just couldn't avoid bringing up the subject. "Bill," I began, "I'm so embarrassed that you saw me roping so bad today. Finally someone I admire so much comes to my clinic to watch me, and then I rope like that."

Bill was always a gentleman. "Aw, don't you worry about it," he reassured me. "I know you can rope because I've seen your videos." He knew I'd had a bad day, and he sure wasn't going to lie to me and tell me that I'd roped well, because I hadn't, but he still found a way to say something nice. He always did.

Gentleman is the word. I once watched him teaching a lady how to rope. He was on his horse holding a calf by the neck with his rope when she threw a heel shot. It was a horrible shot, the most pitiful wad of garbage you've ever seen thrown. And the lady knew it, too.

But Bill just looked at the lady and he said, "Boy, I would have thought that would have gone under a lot better than that."

The lady was so appreciative that Bill had been kind to her, I wouldn't be surprised if she loved him forever. And, of course, that got to be the running joke among us cowboys. Whenever one of us would throw a bad shot, we'd say, "Boy,

I would have thought that would have gone under a lot better than that."

Among the horsemen I've the pleasure to work around and whom I've tried to pattern my life after have been, of course, Ray Hunt, Bill Dorrance, and his brother Tom. Out of the English riding world is George Morris, former Olympic medal–winning show jumper and now a leading trainer of jumpers. He's quite a horseman in his own right.

Many other cowboys and individuals I've met over the years have influenced me in one way or another, even though they didn't have well-known names. They've taught me to think things through, especially the preparation and the follow-through.

And they've taught me to listen, not just to them and to other people, but to the horses I want to help and that want me to help them.

5
The Fall

A S I CONTINUED MY CAREER at Spanish Creek, I rekin-dled a relationship that would have a major impact on my life. It all began in 1981 when I was working as a cowboy for the Three Forks Ranch. I got a call from a woman named Cathy Tamke, who was putting on a fashion show for a ski company at a hotel near Helena. She offered me $150 to do some rope tricks for the show.

One hundred and fifty dollars to do fifteen minutes of rope tricks was big money, so I made the hour-and-a-half drive to the hotel. When I met Cathy at the hotel, she introduced me to her friend named Adrian Logan. Adrian was a very beautiful woman.

They took me backstage to a dressing room so I could change into my red-white-and-blue Tom Mix–wanna-be trick-roping outfit. The room was full of gorgeous models, and if there were any other men there, I didn't notice.

I was nineteen years old at the time, in the middle of beautiful girls running around in their bras and panties. Some of them didn't have any clothes on at all. I was trying to be a gentleman and not look, but let's not forget that I was only nineteen. It took me the longest time to get dressed. The place was as close as I've come to the *Playboy* mansion.

Cathy came in and got me, and I went out and did my rope tricks. I did the usual Texas Skip, the One Hand Stand, and the Pop Over. I also did the Double Merry-Go-Round, which requires two ropes: it involves changing the right loop to the left hand and the left loop to the right hand, and then doing it all behind your back. At the time only two people in the history of trick roping had ever done it. Will Rogers was one, and I was the other. The audience applauded and whistled and screamed, and that was quite a thrill for me.

Afterward Cathy, Adrian, and I went out for a bite to eat. Adrian was a blonde, three years older than me. She was real witty, too, with a comeback for anything or something else cute to say. Plus, her dad was Pete Logan, a famous rodeo announcer, and she had been around ranches and the rodeo business forever. I did whatever I could to charm Adrian. Although she knew I was interested in her, she also knew Cathy was attracted to me, so she remained pretty standoffish.

I didn't see Adrian again until the fall of 1984 when one day she just walked into the arena in Gallatin Gateway where I was riding horses. I couldn't have been more surprised. She was a student at Montana State, and she was looking for a place to keep her horse. She was also interested in the training methods I was using. At that time she was engaged to marry a world-champion bronc rider named Clint Johnson, who was using these methods, too, on his own saddle horses. Kevin Stallings, a good hand from South Dakota and a friend of Clint's, had mentioned to Adrian that I'd quit doing rope tricks and was using the new methods as well. That's when Adrian decided to look me up.

It was a cold day, but the stall barn was warm, and we sat and talked for a couple of hours. We really hit it off. Her interest in hanging around made me start to think that maybe I had a chance with her after all. I was amazed. I'd never have thought that a girl like that would have given me a second thought.

I had been studying accounting at Montana State off and on, and I was thinking about going back for the winter quarter. Knowing Adrian was a student cinched it.

We got to be good friends at school, and we spent quite a bit of time together. We had a lot of fun, and I helped her with her horse. Adrian really liked to ride; she had good balance and a pretty good feel for a horse. She really liked horses, which meant quite a lot to me.

Adrian broke off her engagement, and we started dating. Shortly after we became serious, she took me home to meet her parents, Pete and Audrey. Pete wasn't very friendly, but I told him that I was honored to meet him and that I had always wanted to work in one of his rodeos. Pete worked the big shows, and even though my trick roping was top level, I had never been in one that size. I told him that I'd have known I'd made the big time if I'd gotten to work in a rodeo that Pete Logan was announcing.

As soon as I said that, Pete decided I was all right. He'd been a legend in the rodeo business, but some of the younger, more outgoing announcers were getting the work now. All legends eventually have to back away and let the younger guys take over; that's where Pete was in his career, and he was a little bitter about it.

The Logans had two boys and another daughter, but Adrian was sort of the son that Pete had really hoped for. He was closer to her than he was to his other kids. They were so close she'd rarely make a move without first checking with her dad. Pete never really wanted Adrian to move away, and neither did Audrey. Adrian was their way of hanging on to their youth, I suppose. The pressure of their possessiveness had ruined Adrian's relationship with a couple of good men before me, but I figured that I could fix about anything, and I hung in there.

Nevertheless, there were times when Adrian's parents encouraged her to go out with other men. I guess I should have seen that early on. Adrian was telling me how much she loved me, but at the same time she was going out with—of all guys—my buddy Jeff.

The three of us were taking classes at Montana State. One night she'd be with me, and the next night she'd be with Jeff. Neither guy knew it until I came by her place unannounced one night. She was living in an apartment on Grand Street in Bozeman, and I was going to take her out for a bite to eat. When I pulled up, I saw Jeff's pickup parked in front. I didn't even bother getting out and going to the door. I just drove away.

When I stayed away for a little while, Adrian finally phoned me to ask why she hadn't heard from me. I told her about seeing Jeff's truck, but she didn't really apologize. She liked both of us and felt kind of torn. She didn't want to hurt either one of us, which sounded like a pretty weak excuse to me.

An old friend told me once, "Any woman who allows two men to fight over her is playing both ends against the middle, and she isn't any good for either of them." He was right, but Jeff and I were like a couple of young bulls. When we found out we were rivals for the same woman, it was a hell of a wreck and it destroyed our friendship for a while. In the end, it would be the thing that strengthened it.

If the same kind of thing happened again, I'd walk away as fast as I possibly could. But at the time, I hung in there, and I guess I won the contest because Adrian broke up with Jeff and continued to date me. Jeff and I went from being best friends to being enemies.

I moved away from Spanish Creek and leased another indoor arena across the valley. I also rented a small apartment in Belgrade, just outside Bozeman, near the new arena. The place was a glorified bunkhouse, with a hot plate, a bed, and a bathroom that I built. Pretty modest digs, you'd have to say.

Still, Adrian moved in with me. She didn't want her parents to know we were living together, so she kept her own apartment where she kept a few clothes. She was always worried about what her parents would think, which in some ways was certainly understandable. But as our relationship developed, I saw she wasn't just close to her parents, she was totally manipulated and dominated by them.

Although Adrian and I talked about marriage, she kept putting off our engagement. Normally it's men who do that sort of thing, but not in this case. It hurt, because I really loved her and wanted to be married to her.

One day I was riding colts when Preacher Dave Edwards came by. Preacher Dave had started a little Baptist church in Bozeman that catered to the cowboy crowd, and Adrian and I had become friends with him. He told me he needed to talk to Adrian and me about our living together. He said that because he loved us both, he thought we ought to think about going ahead and getting married because living together wasn't right. He knew we weren't raised that way.

Preacher Dave must have been right because after he put us on the spot, Adrian and I started talking about marriage. Over the next few days, we talked about it a little bit more.

Adrian said she didn't want to have a regular wedding; she didn't want to make a big deal out of it. My guess was that she was afraid her folks would be angry and wouldn't come. She didn't even want Preacher Dave to marry us; instead, she suggested a justice of the peace.

I was very disappointed. I wanted our wedding to be a big deal. I was so proud of her, I wanted all my friends to come and share my happiness. On the other hand, if we were going to get married, it only would happen her way.

We took out a marriage license, and one morning we decided we'd drive over to Broadwater County near where her parents lived and get married by the local justice of the peace.

Adrian called her parents and said, "We're going to do it, and we'd like you to be there." Although the justice of the peace was just a fifteen-minute drive away, they refused to come. That really upset Adrian. We drove into town, and she cried all the way. I told her, "Adrian, if you don't want to do this, let's just stop and forget it. I'll turn the truck around, and we won't."

She shook her head. "No, go ahead. We need to do this. Keep driving."

God knows why I didn't turn around, but I didn't. I was under the impression that Adrian, who was now twenty-seven years old, had decided she finally needed to take charge of her life and make a decision without her parents.

Adrian continued to cry. I felt terrible, too, but we went through with the ceremony. The justice of the peace did the honors, and a couple of total strangers were witnesses.

None of my family was there either. Betsy Shirley, my foster mother, who had raised me through some tough times, was very disappointed. When I called and told her what had happened, she said she understood, but it would have been a special thing for her to be at the wedding.

Afterward, Adrian wanted to go to her parents' house and visit them for a minute. Although seeing them was the last thing in the world I wanted to do, I wanted my bride to be happy.

You would have thought I had committed murder in the first degree. The Logans made me feel like a criminal. Rather than being happy for her, they acted as if somebody had died. It was like a funeral, dead quiet.

I had my own business and was getting to be successful. I didn't depend on anybody for anything, and I loved the Logans' daughter to death, but that wasn't enough for them. They had plans for her.

At one time, Adrian had been dating Montana's secretary of state, a man who was being touted as the next governor until he was killed in a plane crash. Adrian had stopped dating him by then, but her parents remained disappointed that she married a cowboy like me. They still had hopes she'd be the first lady of Montana, I suppose.

As Adrian walked out to the truck, Pete held me back. With a begrudging handshake, he said, "You better do this right, or I'll kill you."

That visit to her parents had done the trick. Ten minutes after we were married, Adrian began to feel she had made a mistake. For my part, I believed that if she came to under-stand how much I loved her and she came to realize she had to leave her parents and cleave to someone else, as the Bible says, then things would work out.

It never happened. Adrian and I got along only all right. We didn't fight, but things never really did improve. I sus-pect Adrian always figured on leaving me. I know for a fact her parents wanted her to. Many years later I found out that even after we were married, they encouraged Adrian to go out on a date with another man.

Adrian didn't go out with him that I know of, but it wasn't for lack of her family's trying. We always spent holidays at their house, and one Easter Adrian's sister Leslie, who was up visiting from Texas, brought up the man's name at the dinner table. All the Logans started talking about how he was probably going to be the next governor, which led to talk about some of Adrian's other past boyfriends. Although I tried to be good-natured about it, I thought the conversa-tion was inappropriate in front of me, but it wasn't my din-ner table.

When Pete said I couldn't be compared to the politician, I lost my temper. "Well, I'll tell you one thing," I said an-grily, "I *can* compete with him as well as anybody because I'm a good man. I try to hold myself up as a good example to other people, and I think I'm a good person, and you can go to hell." That marked the first time I ever stood up to Adrian's father. As I got up to leave the table, I told Adrian that she could stay if she wanted to, but I was going home.

Even though they didn't apologize, the Logans asked me to stay, and I calmed down enough to finish dinner. There wasn't much talk for the rest of the meal, and when it was over, I left. Adrian didn't. She said she'd be home in a few days, so right then and there I found out where her loyalties were.

Adrian did return two or three days later. For the next couple of years we stumbled along, even with lots of good times. Adrian liked riding colts and helping me out, and the business was starting to grow. I was settled into doing some clinics, and I was riding a lot of colts. We bought twenty acres and a doublewide trailer house in a pretty spot near Belgrade. It was the first time I ever owned anything substantial in my life. Granted, it was just a trailer house, but it was brand new, and it beat the hell out of the bunkhouses I'd been living in.

For the next several months I rode colts like crazy. I rode fifteen a day, every day, until I had our little place paid for.

Just one week after I'd made that final payment, Adrian and I were loping horses around a tilled track that circled our little slice of heaven. The date was October 18, 1987. I had stopped the colt I was riding for a breather, taking the time to enjoy the red-and-orange sunset over the Tobacco Root Mountains. Adrian and I were to have dinner with Allan and Jood, friends who had come in from California, and I was about to put my colt away and start the evening feeding.

After riding hundreds of horses in my life, I'd gotten used to the sound of hoofbeats. I knew what they should sound like, and the ones coming from behind me didn't sound right. I looked around just in time to see Adrian and her gelding, Rooster, falling to the ground. They seemed to be falling in slow motion. I was off my colt and running toward her before she landed.

For some reason, Adrian didn't put her arms out to break her fall. Her head slammed into the ground. When I got to her, she was unconscious. She wasn't breathing, and her heart had stopped.

I yelled for help, and Jood ran out of the barn. Fortunately, Jood knew CPR, and as she worked on Adrian, I ran inside to call an ambulance.

Although the local hospital arranged for a flight to the trauma center in Billings, the doctors told me they were pretty sure Adrian wouldn't live through the flight. Ninety percent of her brain had hemorrhaged, and even if she made it to the hospital alive, the swelling would likely kill her within a day or two.

Adrian was in a very deep coma and put on life support. She was at what the doctors call a level eight, which is non-responsive. The neurologist was blunt about it. He told me on several occasions, "I can't give you any good news. I can't even tell you that she's going to live. In fact, I'm surprised she's lived this long."

I spent the next seven weeks by Adrian's side. I slept in my clothes in her hospital room for the first few weeks, and then I stayed in Billings on the living room couch at a place that belonged to the daughter of a friend from Belgrade.

My insurance was not enough to cover all the medical bills. Plus, I had other expenses. I fell way behind because I wasn't working. When I ran out of money, Tom Dorrance and some of my other California friends put together a benefit clinic in Malibu on my behalf. The event gave me the money to live on while I was by Adrian's side in the hospital.

The frustration was awful. I missed Adrian horribly, but I couldn't talk to her. There was nothing I could do to help her. It was the same kind of frustration I had experienced when my mother died, and in my misery I got a tiny glimpse of what my father might have felt.

The Logans spent lots of time at the hospital, too. Their beautiful daughter had been hurt, and since it seemed as if they had to resent somebody, they resented me. I couldn't tell if they blamed me for the accident or if they just hated me because I married Adrian and took her away from home.

They didn't mince words. When I'd walk into the hospital room, Audrey would look at me and ask, "What are you doing back here? She never wanted to be married to you."

It wasn't true, of course, but it didn't matter to me then. Adrian's getting well was all that mattered.

Weeks went by, and I sat with Adrian every day. The only times I wasn't by her bed and talking to her to try to make contact, I was in the hospital chapel praying like I'd never prayed before. Desperation makes for a religious man. Seven weeks went by, but there was still no sign of improvement. It seemed there was no hope.

A constant stream of people came by to tell me how much they loved me and cared for me. They all gave me a lot of support. Allan and Jood and Preacher Dave were there. Chas Weldon, the saddlemaker, came by, and so did Bob Mulkey, and my friends Bob Potts and Greg Eliel. Ray and Caroline Hunt called, and so did the Dorrance family. I wasn't alone, but it was a very lonely time.

I was in the hospital's waiting room when a phone call came from Jeff. The last time I'd seen him, I wanted to beat the hell out of him because I felt that he'd taken advantage of our friendship. I'm sure he felt the same way. I can only imagine what he must have gone through deciding whether or not to call after he heard about Adrian. But he did call, and I was grateful. We talked a little bit, and a few days later he visited me at the hospital. A lot of what had seemed so important in the past no longer mattered now, and continuing to harbor the bitterness and anger that I had felt was now senseless. Jeff and I spent time together and rebuilt our friendship, both of us realizing that the reason our friendship had ended was the reason we were friends once again.

Betsy rarely went into Adrian's room. She felt that Pete and Audrey resented her, too, if only because she was my foster mother. She waited in the hall or in the waiting room for me. When I came out for a few minutes' breather, she would give me a reassuring hug. Betsy was almost seventy years old at the time, and the days she spent at the hospital were hard on her, too.

At nine o'clock one night during the eighth week, Jood came by to help out. I had run out of strength and hope, and while Jood stayed with Adrian, I went down to the chapel. I got down on my knees and said, "God, You've been listening to me for a long time, and I've given all I've got. I feel like I'm used up. I don't have anything left. All I ask is that You just give her a chance—give us a chance—that we might get our lives back, and that I might talk to my wife . . . my friend again. I don't know if You really give signs, but I need one now."

I sat there for a long time, feeling sorry for myself, and lonesome, too. Then feeling a little guilty for trying to tell God what I thought He ought to do, I went back up to Adrian's room.

As I walked in, Jood looked at me and asked, "Where were you two minutes ago?"

"Down in the chapel," I replied. "I was just praying, asking God to give us a break."

"Well, you got your break," Jood said. "Two minutes ago Adrian's eyes opened and she squeezed my hand. She didn't look at me, but her eyes did come open."

Adrian started to regain consciousness. She became aware of things, but only on a very basic level. At first she didn't recognize me. One of her doctors, a woman named Morstad, suggested that I go home and get her wedding ring, on the possibility that seeing it might eventually help Adrian remember she was married to me. I didn't want to leave the hospital, so I asked a friend to get it, and when it came I put it on Adrian's hand.

Whenever the Logans came to visit, I left them alone so they could have private time with their daughter. They told her she was not in love with me and had made a mistake in marrying me.

And because Adrian's memory of her parents was long term, she recognized them long before she recognized me. To her, I was just a friendly guy at the hospital who was taking her to her different therapies, cheering her on, helping her in and out of her wheelchair, washing her, changing her diapers, and getting her ready for bed at night. She still didn't know I was her husband, so I wasn't much competition for her parents.

The doctors had suggested that Adrian not be asked to deal with adult situations or be expected to be capable of adult reasoning and thinking. In short, they asked me not to put any sort of demands on our relationship. They knew full well that Pete and Audrey were trying to turn her against me, and although the doctors advised them against it, the Logans weren't listening. Adrian was very childlike when she came out of her coma, which the Logans seemed to appreciate. Manipulating their little girl was much easier than misleading the adult woman who had made the decision to marry a cowboy like me. They wanted their daughter back home again, and this was an opportunity to tear her away from me.

Before the accident, Adrian was never foul-mouthed, she never swore, but when she came out of the coma she could put a truck driver to shame. Her recovery wasn't like in the movies, where someone wakes up out of a coma and gives you a big hug just before the closing credits roll. When Adrian wasn't hollering and swearing, she was a wild animal, screaming and making no sense. It was as if a bunch of tape players were all going at once, as if thousands of words were coming out of her mouth at the same time. Every thirty seconds or so, I'd hear a word that I recognized. Adrian's mind was so jumbled up, it seemed as if she was possessed by the devil.

The pain and despair of being the spouse who had not been hurt began to make me question my own sanity. I'd rather have been dead than to see Adrian go through what she was going through. If I could have traded places with her, I would have. And I know that if I had been able to trade places, I wouldn't have been alone. My friends and my family would have been there for me.

Adrian spent nearly three months in rehabilitation. Minute by minute, day by day, her recovery continued. She had a busy schedule. Every day she'd go from occupational therapy to physical therapy to speech therapy. I pushed her wheelchair to each session. When I could help the therapists by taking part, I did. Sometimes I was the cheerleader, and sometimes I was the therapist. The doctors wanted me to take part as much as possible because they were trying to help her remember me and remember what we were.

It wasn't easy. When you look at someone you love so much, your best friend, and she is finally able to speak again, and her voice sounds like it used to, as if she'd never been hurt, and you look in her eyes and see hate, and when she looks back at you and she says, "I hate you, I wish you would never, ever come back," it's hard. And then when a minute later she says, "I love you so much. Thank God you're here, I couldn't do it without you," that's hard, too.

The entire time Adrian was in rehabilitation, her parents tried to convince her to go home with them rather than stay with me. They knew why the wedding ring was back on Adrian's hand, and they didn't want her to remember she was married to me. And since the ring didn't mean anything to the Logans, they convinced her sister Leslie to take it off her hand.

By the time I saw the ring was missing, Leslie and her parents had already gone back to the apartment they had rented in Billings. I knew what had happened. I went to their apartment, and when Leslie answered the door, I asked, "Where's Adrian's ring?"

She said, "I don't know what you're talking about."

"I want her ring, and I want it now." I knew she was lying.

Leslie knew she was caught. "I'm not going to give it to you."

Pete and Audrey came to the door. I knew Pete carried a gun in his coat pocket; he'd told me he did. He had his hand on it now.

I looked at him and lost my temper. "You better not pull that gun out of your pocket unless you plan on using it because I'm going to shove it up your ass."

Audrey jumped in front of husband and pushed him back out of the doorway. "Pete, don't do it."

"You better not, Pete," I continued, "because if your wife can hold you back, you don't want any part of me." I turned to Leslie, "This is not the end," I said and walked away.

A few days later Adrian left the hospital. She left me, too. The day she got hurt, we were as close as we had ever been, but the person she was before the fall no longer existed. During her recovery she and I hung in there and saw it through, all the tough parts and the tougher parts. She did great, but it wasn't enough.

Still, as I helped Adrian into her parents' car, she told me, "I'm just going to go home to get well."

Perhaps she genuinely believed she would come back to me, but I told her, "Adrian, you aren't responsible for what you're saying right now. You don't understand what you're saying. I know your parents will never let you leave. In a few days, they'll have you convinced that I'm some kind of monster. This will probably be the last time I ever tell you that I love you, and it'll probably be the last time we ever see each other."

A week later, I was served divorce papers. I lost everything. Our house and twenty acres, the barn and corrals that I'd built were all gone—my few assets were added to the Logan estate.

I had no money, but my bills were paid and I had a little time before the divorce became final and I had to get out of the house. My response was to hide. I stayed indoors with the door locked and shades pulled down, watching TV and drinking coffee. I didn't talk to anyone.

After two months of such mourning, I woke to a sunrise much the same color as the sunset I remembered October 18. I got up, walked out to my round pen for the last time, and stepped onto a horse. And as the sun rose, so did my spirits. It was time to live again.

I drove out of that part of my life with only a pickup truck and a horse trailer. For most of that spring I just kind of bounced around, hanging out with Jeff and his dad and some of my other Flying D friends and helping out with sorting cattle and branding. I did a couple of clinics, which kept me going part of the time, but I wasn't really going anywhere in particular until later on that summer when I went to work for Jorie Butler Kent's polo operation.

Later that year I got a letter from Adrian. She sounded as if nothing had really happened. It was as though the way she divorced me hadn't devastated me financially, hadn't taken everything I had ever worked for. She didn't come right out and say it, but reading between the lines it seemed as if she was trying to patch things up. She did say she wanted to hear from me, but by then it was too late. The pages had already been turned on that chapter in my life.

6
Welfare

ONE OF THE MOST INTERESTING and important horses in my life was named Bif.

He came into my life during the summer of 1988. I was in despair over the ending of my first marriage, and I had been looking for months for ways to save myself. Once I started working with Bif, however, things began to look up. He was an important turning point in my life, and I damn sure was in his.

Because Bif was a dangerous horse to be around—he was lethal with his feet—I had to put so much of myself into working with him, not just to succeed, but to survive. It was hard to figure at the time, but Bif was quite a gift to me, all part of the healing process. He was also a validation of the approach to training horses that I had become associated with.

I named him Bif after Marty McFly's nemesis in *Back to the Future,* a popular movie at the time. The movie Bif was a big, tough, violent sort of person. ("Bif" was also an acronym for "Big Ignorant Fool," something my friends came up with when I started working with the horse.)

Bif had belonged to a horse outfit on the Madison River in Montana, an outfit that had a reputation for raising tough horses, broncs that tended to have problems with people. Rodeo stock contractors who knew about the horses figured anything with that outfit's brand had a pretty good chance of making a good bucking horse, a real draw at rodeos.

I was working on the other side of the river at the time, and I had been watching the outfit's cavvy of horses for several weeks. Bif stood out from the bunch. He was a big red thoroughbred-type Quarter Horse, and I knew he had some age on him—he looked to be four, maybe five years old. I needed a good gelding for the clinics I gave, so one day I rode across the Madison for a closer look.

The horse had a head that only a mother could love, and then only with a little effort. I could see he was pretty troubled and pretty scared. And I knew the reason why.

The folks who owned him had their own way to halter-break their horses. They'd put them in tie stalls and man-handle the halters on. This wasn't too hard to do when the horses were babies and were in tie stalls that measured only twelve by twelve feet. Then the horses would be kept tied up and away from food or water, sometimes for long periods of time, so that when they were untied, the young horses would readily lead to the stream to drink.

Even though the people had the best of intentions, the treatment was rough, and what came next was worse. Instead of teaching the horse how to give to pressure, one man would pull on his head as another one whipped him from behind. That's because the people thought the horse would associate getting a drink of water with leading. I don't know which brain trust thought this up, but it lacked a little in the logic department, not to mention how unkind it was.

You can only imagine the wrecks that resulted. Some horses couldn't handle the pressure, and when they'd try to pull away, they'd flip over backward. They'd begin kicking and striking and biting at the rope, with their ears pinned back.

Unfortunately, a lot of people still use this primitive method. They muscle their horses around and give "cowboys" a bad name.

Bif had been "trained" to lead this way. He'd also been branded and castrated during this time. Everything that had been done to him had been negative, and as far as he was concerned, humans were the enemy. But Bif was a survivor. His spirit didn't bend, and so rather than work with him, the horse handlers simply turned him out to pasture for a long period of time. This was a bad move all around. It meant he got to dwell on his negative exposure to humans.

That was the way Bif came back in from pasture when I met him. I could tell that he'd pretty much decided nothing like his past was ever going to happen to him again. But I still liked what I saw, and, after some thought, I bit the bullet and made the deal to buy him. I basically paid what is called "canner price," what the dog-food people would have paid.

The folks in the outfit ran him into a big pen, and I rode in on my saddle horse and roped him. I thought I'd try to lead him into the horse trailer, but at the time I didn't realize just how unhalterbroke he was.

There was a bunch of activity as we were getting the trailer positioned, and I had Bif stopped with the rope around his neck. I needed to check on the truck, so I asked someone in the corral to hold on to Bif. "Don't pull on him at all," I said, "just hold the rope, and keep it from getting down in the manure." The corrals at this outfit were really dirty, and the manure and mud were a couple of feet deep.

As soon as I started to walk away, Bif felt pressure from the rope and flipped over backward four times within about sixty seconds. It was awful. I ran back and got the rope off Bif's head, then urged him into the trailer free, just as you would load a cow.

As I hauled Bif away, I reflected on what a potential idiot I was for getting myself into another "project." I just couldn't have picked a nice easy one. Oh no, I needed to prove something.

When we got home, I chased Bif into an indoor round corral. A round corral is essential to the kind of training I do because there are no corners where a horse can run and hide. A round corral allows a horse to know that there is no place he can go where he can't move forward, no place where he can stop and lose his energy.

Bif stayed down at the west end, walking in and out of shafts of afternoon sunlight. I took a deep breath and walked toward him. Holding the tail of my halter rope, I tossed the halter harmlessly on the ground behind him. I was hoping he'd move his feet and step away, which would be a beginning. That's because a cornered horse instinctively moves his hindquarters toward whatever is threatening his safety. He stops his feet and prepares to kick (some studs will present their front end to be able to bite as well as rear up and strike with their forefeet).

To encourage a horse to overcome this instinct, you must show him that he can move his feet forward without feeling as if he's surrendering any of his defense mechanisms. He must also see that he can turn his head and look behind him with either eye; he needs to see you without feeling that you are going to take his life.

You then want to draw the horse's front quarters toward you. Getting him to turn his head and look at you is the preliminary step to his hindquarters falling away so the front end can come toward you (we call that untracking the hindquarters).

Looking at you is the equivalent of shifting into neutral, presenting himself in such a way that he's exposing his head to possible risk. You've not won him over yet: he's tolerant but not accepting. It's as though the horse still has a pistol, but he's lowering it instead of pointing it at you. In other words, you've climbed a small hill. You haven't climbed the mountain yet, but you've made a good start.

At this point, Bif saw me the same way he saw every other human. He figured I wanted to end his life, and he was going to make sure that didn't happen even if it meant taking mine. So instead of stepping away from the halter, he started kicking at it. Then he started kicking at me. He'd actually run backward at me and fire with both hind feet. This was quite a sight, especially from up close.

He'd kick at me and miss, and kick some fence boards out of the corral. After a while there were splintered boards all over the place, like piles of kindling.

I spent the next ninety minutes reeling the halter in, and tossing it back at Bif's hindquarters, trying to encourage him to move his feet forward and not be so defensive. It took that long before I got one single forward step.

After another hour and a half, Bif was taking a few steps forward, then a few more, and it wasn't too long after that before I was driving him around the corral. That's not to say I could walk up to him. When I did, he'd try to paw me on top of the head or kick me. He wasn't a lover quite yet.

When working with a horse, particularly a troubled horse, you'll notice that he will spend a good portion of his time avoiding contact, physical and mental. By causing him to move, and then moving in harmony with him, you will slowly form a connection, as if you're dancing from a distance. Yet the horse may remain quite wary of you. When the distance between you and the horse becomes comfortable to him, you start to draw him in. You do this by moving away as he begins to acknowledge you with his eyes, ears, and concave rib cage (middle of rib cage arched away from you). At this moment you and the horse are "one." The farther you move from him, the closer he moves to you. This is known as "hooking on," and it's an amazing feeling. It's as if there is an invisible thread you're leading the horse with, and there's no chance of breaking it.

Before that first evening was over, after I'd spent about four hours in the corral, I finally did move up to Bif. That's when I was able to get him to "hook on" to me. He'd turn and face me, and then he'd walk toward me with his ears up. We were now making positive physical contact. What I was doing with Bif was similar to what Forrest had done with me on the day we met, the day he gave me the buckskin gloves. He didn't force his friendship on me. He maintained a comfortable distance until I was ready to come to him.

The experience also reminded me how much preparation and groundwork people need in order to give their horses—and themselves—a good foundation. They need to work on using the end of the lead rope to cause the front quarters and the hindquarters of their horses to move independently, whether the horse is moving forward or backward, right or left. The horse needs proper lateral flexion so that he can bend right or left while moving his feet at the same time. Horses need to be able to bend and give and yield, just as experienced dancers are able to bend and yield to their partners' lead.

Working a horse on the end of a lead rope, you may see tightness or trepidation when you ask him to move a certain way or at a certain speed or when using his front or hindquarters. Whenever you see it, you home in on that area until the horse becomes comfortable. Then you move on to something else. Just as important, through the directional movement that you put into the end of the lead rope, you can show the horse that he can let down his defenses, that he can move without feeling troubled, without feeling that he needs to flee. Rather than leave you, he can go with you, and both of you can dance the dance. Sometimes the music plays fast, sometimes it plays slow, but you must always dance together.

As long as I did it in a way that was fitting to Bif—that is, very, very carefully—I could touch him and rub him. One little wrong move on my part, and he'd have pawed my head off or kicked me in the belly. But I had to touch him, because that established the vital physical and emotional connection between horse and human. I rubbed him with my hand and with my coiled rope along his neck, rubbing him affectionately, the way horses nuzzle each other out in a pasture and especially the reassuring, maternal way a mare bonds with her foal.

I also rubbed Bif with my rope and my hands along his back and his flanks. That not only felt good to him, but it introduced him to the pressure he would feel when the saddle was on and the cinch was tightened.

When I got Bif saddled up later that night, he put on a bucking demonstration like you've never seen. The stirrups were hitting together over his back with every jump. Watching him, I knew that if he bucked with me on his back, there was no way in the world I would ever be able to ride him, so I didn't even try. I just tried to get him a little bit more comfortable with a saddle on his back, then I unsaddled him and put him up. We ended on a good note, and I wanted him to sleep on it.

I was awake all night trying to figure out how I could help this horse. The next day I repeated the process. Bif was still very defensive, but we gained ground more quickly, to the point where I could step up on him and ride.

Bif never did buck with me. On the ground, he was one of the most treacherous horses I've ever been around, but it was because that bunch of hairy-chested macho cowboys got him started off on the wrong foot. With horses, as with people, you get only one opportunity to make a good first impression, and they missed theirs.

For the next couple of years I hauled Biff to my clinics, but I had to make sure people didn't get near my horse trailer. He'd have kicked or struck them before they knew they were within his range. Even if I was sitting on him, people had to keep their distance. Bif was sure of me, but he wasn't sure of anybody else. I could ride him, but that didn't mean he was gentle.

But for all that, whenever I'd leave Bif alone or in an unfamiliar setting, he'd whinny for me. Not the way a horse anticipates or asks for his feed or a treat, but the way an anxious horse calls out to its herd, its source of safety. Bif just didn't want to be without me. He'd always nicker, and it became a special thing between us.

Miles together can change things, and in time Bif got a lot better around people. Now, roughly ten years later, he's so gentle you'd never know that he had the kind of past he

Buck and Bif.

had. Bif's pretty much retired. I use him on the ranch once in a while, and sometimes my little five-year-old daughter, Reata, and I take him for a ride. He's had a good life, and he'll always have a home with me. He's got a heart the size of all outdoors.

I'll never be able to repay Bif for what he's taught me about working with horses. He represents a lot of horses and people, too, who simply got a bad deal at the start. He proves to me that you don't give up, and that even if you're going through something that makes you think your life is over, you can still have a future.

I travel all over the country and get an opportunity to see lots of different people, and lots of different lifestyles and ways of doing things. All in all, I'm actually pretty optimistic about the human condition. I think of all the people who are unfortunate, who don't have good jobs, or who are on welfare. Granted, some of these people are just lazy, and even though they could work, they won't. Maybe they weren't raised right, or maybe they weren't influenced by the right set of circumstances or the right person. But there are other people who aren't lazy and who do want good jobs, and for them, welfare can help. Some of these people prevail despite a rough start and end up with successful lives. There are Bifs all over.

I'm often asked about a welfare program for wild horses called Adopt-a-Horse. It's been quite a hot issue in the

West, where a lot of people on both sides are trying to do the right thing.

Nobody wants to see wild horses disappear from the western landscape. The activists who regard them as indigenous and want to protect them all certainly don't. Neither do most ranchers, some of whom consider the horses to be simply feral. Although the media paints the rancher as the great Satan because he's in favor of culling the wild herds, the rancher is not a bad person. His concern is overgrazing. He wants all animals to have enough to eat, including his cows. Most real ranchers love horses, and they love the free-

Buck shows how calmly a young sale horse responds to his "big loop" demonstration at the Dead Horse Ranch Sale in New Mexico.

dom that the wild horse represents. They just don't want to see the population become so large that the animals will starve to death.

In their infinite wisdom and in an attempt to resolve the issue, the Department of the Interior's Bureau of Land Management (BLM) created the Adopt-a-Horse program. Government officials started rounding up wild horses and holding them in concentration camp–like environments called feedlots, where they were made available for adoption by anyone who wanted a horse.

The BLM thought this would satisfy both the ranchers who wanted a solution to the problem of overpopulation and overgrazing and the activists, mainly people from towns, who wanted to prevent the horses from going to slaughter.

Although the BLM was trying to do the right thing, Adopt-a-Horse didn't work. Allowing people without any qualifications to own a horse, much less a wild one, put lives in danger. That's an injustice to both the horse and his owner. If the horse hurts an owner, the animal gets the blame.

The BLM also created a program in which prisoners are given the opportunity to work with captive wild horses. They gentle them and get them to the point where they are ridable. This is an excellent idea. People who want to own a horse, especially those who have no experience with horses, are a whole lot safer. The horses don't end up in a can of dog food, and the prisoners learn skills that can benefit them when they're released. If nothing else, they're doing something they can feel good about.

I have hope for these wild horses. They are a part of the American West that most people want to see survive. Most of you who are reading this book feel a deep-down ancient bond, a connection between yourself and horses.

7
Down
the Road

THE FIRST CLINIC I EVER DID was in 1983 in Four Corners, Montana, at an indoor arena owned by Barbara Parkening, the wife of Christopher Parkening, the famous classical guitarist. She had a little group of four or five lady friends who all rode together. I'd started a couple of colts for Barbara's brother-in-law, Perry, and he had been trying to get me to give them a horsemanship class.

As this point in my life I was really shy about talking to people in public. I didn't mind performing—my rope-tricks career proved that—but I didn't feel comfortable speaking to groups. Even when I was riding colts, I didn't like people coming around and watching me. They made me nervous. I didn't want the social interaction because it scared me. All I wanted was to be left alone with a pen full of horses.

Perry kept encouraging me, telling me that I had a lot to offer and that I'd do fine in a public situation. I had gotten to know and trust him, so finally I offered him a deal. "All right," I said, "I need maybe a dozen people to make it work. If you get everything lined up, if you make all the arrangements, collect all the money and rent the indoor arena, I'll do the clinic." I figured that if I gave Perry all of the responsibility and I didn't take any interest at all in the deal, he'd just forget about it.

That's not what happened. Perry came back a week later with the news that he had the people signed up, he'd collected the money, and he'd rented the arena I wanted.

Since Perry had done what I'd asked him to do, I had to be good to my word. I showed up and put on a clinic, but to be honest, I don't know if anybody learned anything. I did what many people do when they first get in the teaching business: I tried to sound as much like the teachers I'd had as I could, parroting things that I'd heard over the years.

That's because I had more confidence in my teachers than I had in myself. I couldn't consider myself an authority, someone with anything to offer, when I'd never done something like this before. I was so unsure of myself speaking to a group of people, let alone teaching them, that I really don't know if they learned anything.

When the clinic was over, a little gray Arab was still in his trailer. One of the students had loaded him because she'd wanted to ride him, but she couldn't get him to back out.

I often tell people that if they can't get a horse to back up on the end of a lead rope in the open, they may have a little difficulty getting him to back out of a trailer. A lot of times

One of Buck's greatest pleasures is to put on clinics with the friends who were there for him when he started his career. Here Buck engages a crowd in Billings, Montana, at a clinic sponsored by his friend and saddler, Chas Weldon (standing at right).

a horse would rather flip over than step down into the unknown.

The horse was terrified to come out. I did the best I could to get him to step six inches back, then step a foot or two forward and another foot back. This was to help him gain some confidence moving forward and back in the trailer before he stepped down.

It wasn't easy, but I finally got him out of the trailer. He didn't hurt himself, but he could have. Then I explained to the woman the mistake she had made in the first place. Rather than loading her horse all the way into the trailer before she was sure she could get him out, she should have had him step carefully into the trailer with his front feet, then had him back up while his hind feet were still on the ground. Doing this procedure a few times would have given him the confidence he needed to back out once he was loaded.

If you ever make the mistake of loading a horse into a trailer without having taught him to back up, the best thing to do is park your truck and trailer inside a corral, leave the back door of the trailer open, shut the corral gate, and go to bed. During the night, the horse will get it worked out. He'll come out. That's the lowest-risk way of getting him out of the trailer.

Or, if you've got just one horse loaded in a two-horse trailer, you could remove the dividers. Even though it's a pretty cramped space, you can often encourage the horse to turn around.

Many people consider loading horses into a trailer as something akin to having open-heart surgery. They know they need to do it, but they'll do everything in their power to avoid it. That's because they don't understand what loading is really all about. It's really quite simple, though: if a horse leads well, if he walks with you wherever you wish to go, he'll load well. It's an act of trust between two beings.

At a clinic in California a few years ago, a lady hired me to do a trailer-loading demonstration with her horse. A couple of handlers walked him down to the arena where I was waiting. Then someone drove her trailer up. A few

No horse is a problem horse; there are only problem people. Of the more than ten thousand horses Buck has started in his clinic career, he has never failed a horse. Here he starts a big warm-blood in Malibu, California.

minutes later, the owner herself showed up driving a Rolls-Royce. She stepped out of it and said, "Mr. Brannaman, I'm the owner of this horse, and I'm the one paying you to trailer-load him. I understand your fee is one hundred dollars. If you're able to load him without too much trouble, I want to make sure I get a discount."

The hackles on the back of my neck raised a bit. Here the woman drives up in a two-hundred-thousand-dollar car, and she's worried about not getting her hundred dollars' worth (if the stories I'd heard about her own trailer-loading expertise were true, she'd never find a vet to stitch her horse up for any less than that).

I said, "Ma'am, if you don't feel like you got your money's worth by the time I'm done, then you don't owe me anything."

I started the horse on the end of the halter rope, shaking the rope just enough to get the horse to move his feet back. I was being as subtle as I possibly could, trying to offer him a good deal. When I didn't get the movement I wanted, I got a little more active with the rope until the discomfort of the swing caused him to back up. The effect of the rope wasn't a lot different from a big horsefly buzzing around his head. The rope made him drop his head and back up, the same way a horsefly would.

Once I laid the foundation of getting the horse to move his feet, I could back him just about anywhere I wanted him to go. After just a little while, he was backing very nicely on the end of a sixty-foot rope. I then fed out the rope's coils and backed him up the ramp and into the trailer. His hind end was all the way in the manger and his head hung out the back door. I even got him to where he would start beside the driver's window of the pickup, walk down alongside the truck and trailer, turn the corner, and back up the ramp on his own.

That's when I put the halter back on the horse and handed him to his owner. "There you go, ma'am," I told her. "I've finished with your horse."

Her eyes bugged out so far you could have knocked them off with a stick. "You never loaded my horse."

"Oh, yes I did, ma'am," I replied and turned around to the crowd. "Did I not load this lady's horse?" Everyone confirmed that I sure had.

Buck's little buckskin gelding, Cinch, has traveled with Buck over the years and become almost as well known as Buck himself. Cinch is retired today on Buck's ranch in Sheridan.

She said, "Well, yes, you loaded him, but you loaded him backward."

I put a puzzled look on my face. "Well, ma'am, you didn't say which way you were looking for me to load him, so I don't know how I was supposed to know." With that, I reached into my pocket and gave her back her check. "You have a good trip home, ma'am. I hope everything goes fine for you and your horse."

The last thing I saw at the end of the day was the horse on his way out of the arena, his butt in the manger and his head hanging out the back of the trailer. As he went out the gate, he whinnied at me as if to say, "Well, thanks. It wasn't really what I expected, but I'm in anyway."

The last I heard, that lady was successfully loading her horse on her own. She was still loading him backward, but she was loading him, nevertheless.

It's kind of like the old saying: Be careful what you ask for; you just may get it.

Loading wouldn't be a problem if leading weren't a problem. I wish I had a dime for every horse I see either dragging his owner along at the end of a lead rope or else being dragged. Or make a right turn by being turned to the left three times. You'd think the person would be embarrassed to death, but he's not. I know I would be.

Problems with leading happen because the basic groundwork is lacking. A horse that has learned to hook on to a human and to free up his feet will follow the person calmly and willingly.

One thing, though: People often lead from the wrong place. They walk either directly in front of the horse or back at the hip. Both spots are blind spots where the horse just can't see you, so no wonder he'll run over the top of you or swing into you and knock you flat. Try to be enough to the side and ahead so he can see you. You should be able to make a right turn and not run over the horse to get there.

And speaking of embarrassment, I can't imagine why people who have to stand on a box to get a halter or bridle on their horse's head aren't mortified to let others see them do it. Any horse that can reach down to graze—and that would be every horse—should be able to lower his head so even the shortest person can put on a halter or bridle.

That's why when I start working with young horses or help older troubled ones, I always rub them along on the neck and around the ears. Comforting and supportive touching around the head means a great deal to them. They'll welcome it and put their heads down for more, even when you have a halter or bridle in your hand.

I also make sure that I don't slam a bit into their mouths. That's a quick way to make a horse head shy.

Okay, one more point in this area: A horse that walks off while the rider is stepping on is a reflection of the owner's weak horsemanship. It puts the rider in a precarious position, and it shows that the rider has lost control. All my horses stand while I mount, and they don't move off unless and until I ask, even if they see other horses moving around.

My horses listen to their rider, and I wouldn't have it any other way.

Nor do my horses leave me when I turn them out in a paddock or pasture. They stand quietly while I remove their halters, and they continue to stand while I leave them. That is, I walk away from them and not the other way around. That way, there's never any spinning around and kicking out, so nobody gets hurt.

Early in my teaching career, I gave a summertime clinic in Scottsdale, Arizona. It was 117 degrees, and the dust in the arena was like flour. Nowadays I wouldn't put horses or people through that torture, but we all suffered along. So did the arena crew, who did the best they could to keep the footing watered.

The horsemanship class had about forty people trotting around on their horses in the dust. The sun was blazing, and about halfway through the class, I suggested that everyone take a break for a few minutes.

One fellow in the class was nicknamed Polack. I felt embarrassed calling him that, but he wouldn't answer to his real name. He liked his nickname; he apparently was quite proud of his Polish heritage. Polack had a sorrel horse that was a little on the volatile side, kind of a hand grenade with a saddle strapped on.

When we took the break, Polack rode up to the edge of the arena with the others, stopped at the fence, hooked a leg over his saddle horn, and tipped his hat back, just like the Marlboro Man posing for a cigarette ad. His wife handed him a container of water, a plastic milk jug with ice in it.

When Polack tipped that jug up and took a big slug of water, the ice hit the bottom of the jug. The young sorrel spun around and left, hell-bent for election. Polack still had his leg hooked over the saddle horn and his hat tipped back, and he was still holding on to this jug. Even though realization and terror overtook him, he couldn't seem to let go of the jug. Having seen a similar move with Ayatollah and my coat, I felt "the pain of my brother."

His horse was at a full gallop now, a red blur across the arena. I quickly turned on my microphone and pleaded, "Drop the jug! Polack, drop the jug! Please, *please* drop the jug!" I repeated my plea again and again as he went down the arena, which was about three hundred feet long and surrounded by a fence made of stout two-inch steel pipe.

Just as he raced by me, the light came on. He looked down at his hand and the idea seemed to register on Polack's face. He dropped the jug. But his horse was still at a full gallop, and even though Polack had dropped the jug, they were so close to that pipe fence, I was sure that he had failed to save himself.

It was my first real heavy year of doing clinics, and there I was in the middle of a boiling arena, dust everywhere, and my first fatality was about to happen. As I prepared for the wreck of the century, both Polack and his horse disappeared in the dust.

A miniature mushroom cloud boiled up over the arena. Then, as the dust slowly began to settle, I just about fell over. I felt like one of those cartoon characters with buggy eyes on big springs.

There was Polack—still on his horse, his leg still hooked over his horn, his hat still tipped back on his head. His horse had made a perfect sliding stop, ending with no more than a quarter inch to spare in front of the fencing. The track on the dusty surface of that arena was the most perfect parallel-lined "eleven" I'd seen in a long time.

Polack turned around and looked at me and said, "Yahoo!" The crowd erupted in applause.

After that averted mess that day, I told Polack he was welcome to stay, but with the kind of luck he had, he really didn't need me. The last I heard, he was still alive and well somewhere in Arizona. I hope his luck holds out for him.

I've heard a lot of people say they'd rather be lucky than good, but not me.

Mike Thomas, a friend who had managed the Madison River Cattle Company before he tired of the Montana winters and moved down to Arizona, set up a clinic for me at the Mohawk arena in Scottsdale. We had quite a large group of people, and as it happened, the manager of an Arabian horse ranch that had canceled one of my clinics the year before was one of them.

I was doing a trailer-loading demonstration on a little Appaloosa mare, leading her off my left shoulder from right

Buck on his saddle horse Jack, answering questions at a clinic. Question-and-answer sessions at Buck's clinics last as long as they last—sometimes long after the sun goes down.

to left and getting her to lead past me while I stood still. Once I had her going smooth and could stop her on the lead rope and then get her to step back, we moved to the trailer, where I started loading her and backing her out.

Each time I prepared to load the mare, I'd give her a little more rope and step farther away, thus widening the gap between the trailer and me. If she chose to go through the gap rather than into the trailer, I'd take a step forward and divert her into it. If I hadn't and she had gotten used to going between me and the trailer, it would have been the equivalent of letting her run me over.

Once the mare was confident loading that way, I worked my way up to the left rear of the trailer. I began loading her on an even longer rope, moving her in an arc from my right to my left. I'd pet her and reassure her, back her out again, play out a little more rope, and lengthen the arc. After a little while, I was standing by the tandem wheel so I was out of her sight when she loaded.

By the time I was able to stand by the truck's side mirror, I had to replace her halter with a thin nylon rope around her neck. The mare was real responsive now, and since she was on forty to fifty feet of rope, anything heavier than the nylon would have made her turn and face me.

I finally got the mare to the point where I could sit in the front seat of the truck and feed coils off the rope out the side window. The mare promptly went to the trailer and loaded, which seemed to really impress the folks at the clinic.

At the end of the day, the manager of the Arabian outfit came up to me. He was very excited about what he had just seen. He said he had an expensive Arab stud that had never had a successful trailer ride, and he asked me if I would load him.

I hadn't forgotten that the manager worked for the folks who had betrayed my trust and put me in a bad spot by canceling that clinic. So I said, "Okay, it'll cost you five hundred dollars." In those days I charged a hundred dollars to load a horse, and this was my way of telling him to go to hell.

He didn't even blink. Instead he asked, "When can you show up?"

I wished I'd asked for five thousand, but I had to be good to my word. The next day after I'd finished my clinic, I drove to the fellow's farm. I figured I needed to get the horse pretty well trained for that kind of money, but I got him loading into the trailer without much of a problem. In fact, I got that stud horse to the point where, turned loose beside a pen of mares, he'd walk away from them and get in the trailer.

One person watching this demonstration was a local used-car salesman who had married into a very wealthy family. He was running off at the mouth with some of the other spectators, and I heard him say, "I bet Brannaman couldn't load our horse."

His wife, who had ridden in one of my public clinics and was interested in my kind of horsemanship, said, "Well, honey, I'll bet you a thousand dollars he can." Then she asked me, "Buck, would you be interested in going partners on this?"

I jumped at the opportunity. "Bring him on."

Their horse was a famous Arab halter show horse imported from Europe for more than a million dollars. In those days when a horse needed to show spirit to win a halter class, in which animation seemed to matter as much as proper conformation did, many trainers and judges confused "spirit" with terror. In order to get the right expression, some trainers kept their horses in tiny stalls and ambushed them in the dark with fire extinguishers so that any sound would provoke a terrified "look of excitement." Another favorite trick was to cross-tie a horse in water and hook electrodes to his neck so that he'd tense up when they hit the switch.

That kind of terror tactics had gotten this horse to the point where he was unsafe to work with or just to be around. His stall door had a double padlock so no one would accidentally walk in on him. His owners had catwalks installed on both sides of his stall. To get him to me, his handlers climbed up on them and used long poles with hooks at the ends to grab his halter. Once they had the horse more or less under control, they chained him from both sides and muscled him into a rented semitrailer. It was no easy job, and it took several hours.

When they got to their destination, the handlers had to use their chains to bring the horse into a small arena surrounded by a low fence. When he immediately broke free and began racing around the arena, I saw how dangerous he was. He wore a halter with a chain shank over his nose, and I could tell that he'd had it on for some time because his nose was terribly scarred.

I entered the arena riding my saddle horse. If I'd come in on foot, he would have attacked me. My first job was to get a rope around his neck so I could control his feet. The fence was so low, if I roped him when he was in a corner, there was a good chance he'd jump the fence and break a leg. Plus, if I missed my shot and he jumped out, he would find himself in the middle of one of the busiest roads in Scottsdale. Neither of the prospects was anything I wanted to think about. Aside from the danger to the horse, I wasn't in any position to pay for my mistakes in those days.

After some fifteen minutes, the horse finally moved to the middle of the arena. The roping gods must have been with me, because I roped him around his neck and got him stopped. However, now I had to keep him at the end of my sixty-foot rope, because any closer and he would have crawled up in the saddle with me.

I worked with him the same way I would work a horse I was teaching to lead, getting him to "turn loose" to me. Occasionally, this horse would give to the rope and put some slack in it. However, feeling any pull caused him to immediately begin ducking his head and thrashing around as if to avoid an imaginary whip. He even got down on his knees, laying his head on the ground and closing his eyes as though having a recurring nightmare of past abuse. To imagine what this horse had been through was painful.

After a lot of sweat and tears for that little horse, I was able—after an hour or more—to bring him close enough that I could slip the halter and shank off without being bitten.

Reaching across my saddle horse, I placed my hands over the Arab's nose and rubbed him where he'd been chafed for so many weeks. His response was to lay his head across my leg up on the saddle and close his eyes. He may not have felt this safe since he'd been with his mother. He'd finally met a human who knew how to be his friend.

He and my horse walked around the small arena, his head still in my lap. There was salt on my chaps from rubbing up against many sweaty horses, so when we would stop, the stallion would affectionately lick my chaps. When I put my hands in his mouth around his lips, he gave me no trouble. He wasn't defensive. He had no plans to strike me, bite me, kick me, or even to leave me.

The Arab was leading well, so at this point I felt safe enough to step off my saddle horse and approach the horse trailer. I was now ready to begin what I had been hired to do, although most of my work had already been done.

Getting the horse to load didn't take very long because we had become partners. I could steer him into the trailer by his tail; I could even pick up three tail hairs and back him out of the trailer without breaking one of them.

The horse became so quiet and relaxed, some in the crowd began to worry that he couldn't win a halter class looking the way he did—without the look of terror that's often confused with what they think is "spirit." Hearing them say that made me realize how hard it was to understand how seeing a horse in a relaxed frame of mind could be any cause for worry. These people were as different from me as any people I'd ever met.

As the little horse stood quietly with his head in my arms, a lady in the crowd who owned a local Arabian farm of her own spoke up. "Buck, now that you've gotten this horse coming around the way you have, when would we be able to start with the whips again? Would we be able to start tomorrow, or would we have to wait till next week?"

She had no idea what she was saying. It was the most bizarre thing I'd ever heard, and from a woman who appeared to be so sophisticated. How could she say something so uncivilized?

I couldn't take it, not after what the little horse been through. "Some of you can go to church on Sunday and claim to be holier than thou, but the other six days of the week you're torturing horses and committing crimes against them. You make me ashamed to be a human being."

But that wasn't all that bothered me. That little horse had made a friend that day. He appreciated what I had done with him—I know he did. Yet I went away with a sick feeling, wondering if maybe I had done wrong. On one hand, I had helped him, but I had also shown him there was something truly good in life that he would always miss.

I later learned that he went back to his same life. In that world of barbarians, defense was his only means of survival, and I worried that I might have taken it away from him.

Even years later, I still wonder if he remembered me, the man in the cowboy hat who for just a few hours had been his friend.

You wonder what a horse knows and how deep it runs.

My brother-in-law, Roland Moore, is a good cowboy. Roland married the Shirleys' daughter Elaine, and was working as a cowboy on The Flying D ranch. When we first met I was only twelve and he was twenty-eight, so due to the age difference, our friendship didn't amount to much at first. I saw him off and on, but it wasn't until I was a little older that we started riding and working cattle together.

When Forrest and Betsy were ready to retire, Roland and Elaine moved in and took over the place. It's called the Cold Springs Ranch now, and they all ran it together until Elaine died in 1999. The Flying D and Spanish Creek have since been sold to media mogul Ted Turner, who started a buffalo-raising operation there.

Roland and I were out on horseback one day after I had started competing in high school rodeos. He looked over at my horse and said, "You know, there's a difference between a rodeo cowboy and a working cowboy. Working cowboys don't use tie-downs or draw reins or any of those gimmicks on their horses."

He was right, of course. I was still a kid and didn't realize that using restrictive tie-downs in rough country could be dangerous: a horse that wore one and then stumbled and fell could have difficulty getting his head back up to regain his balance.

During the winter of 1988 when I was in Florida playing polo, Roland called me up. He had acquired a new horse, a palomino named Tony that was a brother to my horse Bif.

According to Roland, Tony was very broncy. "He bucked me off at this branding, and I landed on the back of my head. It felt like he almost broke my neck. I'm going to get rid of him. What do you think about that?"

Now, Roland was about as subtle as a pool cue in a pencil box. I knew he was fishing for me to validate his decision, so I said, "You know, you're probably right, Roland. You don't need a horse like that around."

Roland was real quiet on the other end of the line, so I paused a second and asked, "Do you think it'll ever cross your mind that maybe there was something in that horse you missed? That there's something that you miss on a lot of horses, and maybe it'll come up again, and you'll have the same thing happen, and have to get rid of another horse?"

Roland still didn't say anything, so I went on. "Ah, you know, really, on second thought, you probably should just get rid of him, and don't worry about it. It probably won't come up again." We visited a little bit, and I hung up.

After I got back to Montana that spring, Roland called again. "Hey, I still have that palomino. There's a horse sale coming up in town, and I thought I'd run him through there. But before I do, maybe I'll come by, if you don't mind, and you could have a look at him. Maybe you could tell me what I missed on him. Then I'll go ahead and get rid of him."

I told Roland to come along, and it was pretty clear when we saddled the horse that he had missed some basic groundwork. There were plenty of things Tony couldn't do with his feet because they weren't freed up. As a result, he was having trouble moving his hindquarters to his right. He should have been able to distribute his weight evenly on all four quarters while moving forward or back, but he couldn't. These movements are basic dance steps that a horse learns at the end of a lead rope, and if he can't do them, there's a very good chance he's going to buck somebody off.

I worked with Tony from the back of my saddle horse for a while until his feet were well freed up. Then I told Roland to get on.

Roland looked over at me like he'd swallowed a fly. "You know, the last time he really bucked me off."

This was coming from a good cowboy who has worked on some of the biggest outfits in the country. Tony had really chilled him.

I said, "Roland, you came by for this moment. You really wanted to know or you wouldn't have kept Tony this long. You've got to trust me here—I wouldn't try to get you hurt."

I was sitting in the middle of the round corral on my saddle horse holding on to the end of the lead rope. I had Tony pointed off so he could take a right circle.

Roland swallowed real hard, but he got on. When I told him to move Tony right on up to the lope, he looked at me and said, "That's where he got me—loping him off on a right lead."

"He's all right, Roland," I reassured. "He's all right. Trust me."

To Roland's credit, he did. Tony responded to his cue by loping off into the prettiest circle you've ever seen. After a minute or so, Roland relaxed and realized he wasn't going to die. He looked bewildered. He didn't say anything, but his eyes were asking, Why am I still alive?

When he finally stepped off Tony, Roland was buzzed. All he wanted to do was talk about it. I stopped him and said, "You know, Roland, we'll have to talk about this some other time, or you're going to miss your horse sale. I don't want to make you late."

Roland headed off to town. He was happy, confused, relieved, and exhausted, and I wasn't surprised when I learned he didn't sell the horse.

Tony was a turning point for Roland. For all the experience that he'd had, Roland had decided to become a student again. Since then, he's worked with lots of horses. He's had his ups and downs, but he worked at it and today he's a true student of the horse.

There are two happy endings to this story: Right now Roland is one of the best hands around. Guys who used to think their abilities were on the same level as Roland's got left behind years ago. Some of the people who were once his equals couldn't saddle his horse now.

And Tony? Tony ended up a bridle horse at Cold Springs, one of the best bridle horses you've ever seen. In our circle that means Tony is what is called "straight up in the bridle." He's a fine horse and a true pleasure for anyone to ride. He will live life to the fullest with Roland. In my world, any horseman who can bring a horse to that level is to be highly exalted.

I've been giving clinics for almost twenty years now, and I've seen some pretty odd things and worked with some pretty odd people. The bunch I had at a clinic near Buckeye, Arizona, was one of the strangest. Some of them were bikers, while the others didn't appear to spend a whole lot of time in town. They looked like desert dwellers to me; I don't know what else to call them. None of them looked like horse people.

By nine o'clock in the morning, while I was trying to help them work with their colts, they sat around dressed in black leather and drinking beer. My teaching isn't real formal, but my clinics are normally taken a little more seriously than they were taking this one. They were all attentive, and they were eager enough, but it seemed as if what they mostly wanted to do was party.

Nonetheless, some of their horses were nice and gentle. One little two-year-old filly was a cupcake, but by the way she tiptoed around, I could tell that she was pretty scared. Not wild, but just scared. She hadn't been handled a lot, so she scooted around the corral the way a lot of youngsters will do to avoid being with you.

When the filly's owner identified herself, I saw what the little horse was bothered about. The owner was a woman in her twenties, and if she didn't outweigh the horse, she came close. I can often guess a person's size just by looking at the size of the saddle on the horse, but in this case the two were nowhere close.

The woman walked over to the filly, whose eyes grew big as saucers. The stirrups were only about a foot and a half off the ground, but the woman couldn't put her foot in without just about tipping the little horse over sideways.

"Why don't you get up on the fence," I suggested, "and I'll see if I can teach the horse to pick you up from there."

She couldn't do it—she literally could not get up on the fence. Some of the spectators who saw her dilemma came over to help. They pushed while the woman pulled, until eventually she was perched precariously on the top rail.

I led the filly over and said, "I just want you to get her used to you. I want you to pet her. Rub her and reassure her and get her used to seeing you from up above. Then once she gets a little more comfortable, I want you to s-l-o-w-l-y slide down on her and get settled. Then I'll lead you around, and we'll take you for a little ride."

The average person would understand my meaning: Take your time—I'll let you know when to get on. Not so this gal. She either flew or fell off that top rail. Either way, she angled a leg over the top of the saddle, dove at that horse, and plopped down on her back.

The poor little filly was practically bowed under by this sudden added weight. But she stood there and looked up at me as if to ask, What in the world just landed on my back?

The woman looked terrified. "You're going to be all right," I told her. "It looks to me like you haven't ridden too many colts, so you just rub on her and I'll hang on to the lead rope and help you get through this."

The woman stared at me. "Haven't rode many colts? Hell, this is my first time on a horse."

You can imagine my surprise. I figured I would have to pull a miracle out of an unmentionable place, but that little filly did the job for all of us. I got on my saddle horse and led her around. The filly stayed right underneath that woman, licking her lips with contentment and doing just fine.

Since everything was looking pretty good, I moved the filly up to a trot. My horse had a longer stride, and I wanted the filly to step out and catch up, but the minute the pace increased, the woman panicked. She bailed off and tried to dive for the fence, but her aim was off, and when she hit the ground, she rolled under her horse.

I didn't know what to do. I couldn't back the horse, and I couldn't lead her forward without the woman being stepped on. All I could see was a wreck ahead.

The filly knew full well that we were all in a bad spot. She just looked down, lifted a hind leg to step over the woman, then lifted the other hind leg and stepped over again. I couldn't believe how high she lifted those legs. The filly never even touched the woman. Once she was clear, she walked on by with as happy an expression as I've ever seen on a horse.

The woman stood up, brushed herself off, looked at me, and said, "Well, that's not too bad for the first ride, is it?"

What could I say? I came up with, "No, that's not too bad for the first ride, but if it's all right with you, maybe you could take a little break and I'll have another rider get on and finish up."

She agreed, relief filling her face. I felt the same way myself. Things worked out fine, and before the clinic was over, the lady was back on her filly and doing okay.

I've often told people who ask if there is a God: "Get around enough people with horses and see what happens. See how they survive in spite of all the things that they do, and you'll become a believer!"

At another clinic, this one in Ellensburg, Washington, a student came with a colt that needed some preliminary work. In those days I charged an extra hundred dollars for horses that weren't halterbroken. If they were real tough to work with, I'd give the owners a hand so they didn't have to do all the work themselves.

This horse was wearing a halter when he got out of the trailer, but he was troubled. By the time the other students were saddled up, his owner still couldn't get near him. The colt was pulling away and showing a lot of resistance at the end of the lead rope, the kind of behavior that generally doesn't occur with a horse that has never been handled. Since he was wearing a halter, it was obvious that somebody had tried to start him and failed. He had cuts, nicks, and scars on his body, too.

I told the owner, "Take your halter off and borrow one of mine. Your lead rope's so long, you're going to get in trouble with it. So put mine on him, and then just go up and pet him."

He replied, "I can't get to this horse. He's going to strike."

When I asked how he got the halter on, the owner lied, "Well, we didn't have any problem at home." It was obvious the guy was just biding his time until I took over; he wasn't about to get close to that horse.

The colt really was dangerous, so we ran him into the round corral, and I roped him from my saddle horse. He would strike at my horse, but we stayed out of his way and after I worked with him quite a while, I roped a hind foot. Although the colt gave to the pressure of the rope, I knew that he would kick, so I had my horse hold him by a hind foot so that he couldn't get his hind leg forward.

That's how I saddled him. Once the cinch was tight, the colt bucked quite a bit. He'd had experience at arranging his body in a way that he could get the most leverage when he tried to get away. That's how I could tell somebody had worked with him; he was looking for certain actions from me that he had experienced at the hands of somebody else. When I'd start to approach him, he'd position himself so that he could kick out with his hind legs or rear up and strike.

I felt really sorry for him, and I wanted him to get through this day just as easy as he could. I slipped my halter on him, let my rope drop off his hind foot, and told him, "You know, big fellow, I'm going to just get you rode the best way I can, and then put you out for the day."

I was going to lead him by me just once or twice, get him to break over his hindquarters, and then I'd step up on him. But when I asked him to lead by, he evidently saw me do something that the people who had tortured him had done.

I'm afraid I had let my guard down. The colt reared up on his hind legs, struck out at me, and pawed me to the ground. He had me down between his front legs, and then he leaned down and started biting and chewing on me.

I rolled up in a ball and just tried not to move. A couple of friends were watching, and they told me later they were getting a little concerned. They said it looked as if I was getting into trouble, and they thought they were going to have to jump over the fence and drive that horse off me. At the time I remember looking their way and thinking, Just how bad does this have to get, fellas?

Anyway, I fared surprisingly well. Once up, I got the colt caught again and tried once more. I thought I'd gotten too far ahead of his shoulder the last time, so I stepped a little farther back and tried to lead him again, but I still hadn't learned. The colt got the drop on me again, whirled away, and had me lined up for a kick.

At this point the best I could come up with was to move right into his tail so all he could do was kind of bump me. That's a good thing to know: The closer you stand to a kicking horse, the less impact the kick will have on you.

I stepped in so the colt couldn't really kick me, but he knocked me down again. His owners had turned this poor horse into a predator. He was no longer a herd animal—he was the hunter, not the hunted. I told myself, "You know, Buck, keep this approach up, and there's not going to be much left of you."

I got back on my saddle horse, roped one of the colt's hind feet again, and worked with him some more. Once the colt knew I had the upper hand and he couldn't get to me, he just lay down on the ground—he "sulled up" with frustration the way a spoiled kid does when he lies down on the floor—and he wouldn't move.

I got off my horse while the colt was still down, and as I was getting ready to pull my rope off his hind foot, he rolled an eye back, looked at me, lifted a hind leg, and kicked me right in the middle of the thigh. Then he lay flat again. He was really something.

The benefit of the doubt I'd been giving him was now completely used up. He was still down on his side, and I muttered, "Horse, there is nothing you can do to me while I'm sitting on your back that you haven't already done to me on the ground." I couldn't wait to get on him. I laid a leg over the top of him, just as you saw Tom Booker do in the movie *The Horse Whisperer,* except this wasn't a gentle horse, and we weren't in a movie.

I rocked the colt up and pulled on the saddle horn. He tried to reach around and bite me while he was still lying down, but I was able to get my leg out of the way. When I nudged him in the ribs with my foot, he got up and off we rode.

It wasn't too long before I had him loping around and being guided pretty well. Within a half hour he found out I was different from the man who brought him. Before the morning was out, he and I were roping colts and moving other horses around. He was operating like a saddle horse. We were on our way.

I later found out his owner used a "hot shot" cattle prod to run him into a metal squeeze chute. Then, while clamped in the chute, the horse had a halter forced on him, after which he was spooked into the horse trailer the same way you'd load a cow. The squeeze chute was how he'd gotten so skinned up. It seemed the owner's plan was to save the extra hundred dollars I charged for horses that weren't halterbroken, and at the same time see how much trouble he could get me into.

The next morning the owner arrived with a different horse. "I want you to know that I'm not scared of that horse I brought here yesterday," he assured me. "I just thought I'd learn a lot more from you if I brought a colt I'd already rode a few times. I won't have any problem getting that other horse rode at home. Because like I told you, I'm not scared."

"That's fine," I replied. "But what you don't realize is that with what I accomplished on your horse yesterday, you could have ridden him today. But you go ahead and ride that colt you brought. That ought to be just fine."

He got his second colt saddled up and ready to go. Everyone else in the class was putting a first ride on their colts. When he got on, his colt didn't put up with him for two minutes before he bucked him off on his head. I call that frontier justice. The guy eventually did get the horse ridden and finished out the clinic, but he didn't make many friends that weekend.

I remember that horse quite often because the experience did sharpen me up. I felt so much sympathy for the abuse and torture he'd suffered before he came to the clinic that I tried to do the minimum. What I did helping him come out the other side was not enough for him and certainly not enough for me. To be honest with you, with the kind of owner he had, I don't think that horse survived.

I've worked with similar horses that went away in the same condition, and it always makes me wish I was in a place where I could save every one of them. At the same time, I learned a lot from them, and a lot of people learned from them as well, so maybe it was worth it in the long run.

As I said, I've thought fondly of that horse lots of times. The best I can do is honor his life by using what I learned from him to help others.

8
Playing Polo

JORIE BUTLER KENT WAS OLD MONEY. At one time Paul, her father, owned most of what is now Oakbrook, Illinois, the corporate headquarters for McDonald's worldwide business. Paul's family also owned a large paper company. Jorie ran their horse operation outside Ennis, which included raising and training the thoroughbreds ridden by her husband, Jeffrey Kent, and others on the Abercrombie & Kent and the Rolex high-goal polo teams. Jeffrey was a *patron,* a Spanish word meaning "team owner." Patrons surround themselves with professional players, mostly from South America, who do just about all the scoring.

If you've never seen a polo match, it's basically hockey on horseback. It can be just as rough, too. The play is so hard and so fast that the four players on each team have to change horses after each chukker, the name for each of the six periods of play. A horse—polo people refer to them as ponies, no matter their size—can play two chukkers at most. Not counting spare horses that fill in for tired or lame ones, each player needs a string of five or six horses.

The manager of the operation was Sherry Merica, who came from around Ennis. She had been one of the local moms all through high school (Smokie and I had gone to school with her kids), and after I went to work for Jorie, she and I got to be good friends.

My job was helping to start the horses. After the horses were started, Jorie took them down to Florida where the teams' players would play them. She tried to get the players to ride in the same manner that I did, without tie-downs, bit gimmicks, or other devices of torture that the players thought were absolutely necessary. Their response was that a Montana cowboy might be able to ride a colt, but he wasn't qualified to educate a polo horse.

I grew tired of hearing that reaction, so in the winter of 1988–89 I finally told Jorie, "If you don't mind, I just might go to Florida and play the horses myself this winter." Jorie thought that was a great idea, and I was pleased to hide from the harsh Montana winter.

The Florida sun was shining when we arrived, and it felt glorious to be warm (it had been snowing in Bozeman the day we left). The town of West Palm Beach was right out of *Lifestyles of the Rich and Famous*. I thought some of the houses were hotels until Jorie told me they were single-family residences.

The first time I visited the Palm Beach Polo Club, I arrived with Jorie in her Bentley. Actually, Jorie and I rode be-

Buck and his brother, Smokie, in front of the horse trailer they took on the road. The house in the background is 3219 North Fourth Street in Coeur d'Alene, Idaho.

Buck and Smokie practicing their rope tricks.

Smokie on his first horse, Running Doe.

Ace Brannaman in Idaho, supervising his sons' roping practice.

Seven-year-old Buck practicing rope tricks in his Whitehall, Montana, home.

At a performance for the Special Olympics: Ace, Eunice Kennedy Shriver, Buck, an unidentified contestant, and Smokie.

Buck and his pal Sampson the bull. Buck taught Sampson to do almost anything a horse could—including lower his head for bridling.

Buck and Smokie at the Shirleys' ranch.

Buck's graduation day from Harrison High School. Buck is flanked by Smokie and his aunt, Anne Annis (left) and his foster parents Forrest and Betsy Shirley (right).

Buck on his horse Billy, doing a Texas Skip in Three Forks, Montana, 1980.

Buck meets the locals on a Friendship Force tour of Japan in 1980.

Buck at the Madison River Cattle Company. It was here that Buck's life as a horseman truly began.

Buck works Bif near Monida Pass, Montana. Bif was a difficult horse to start, but a close kinship developed between the two.

Although Buck's venture into the game of polo was mainly inspired by the attraction of warm Florida weather, he nevertheless rose to the occasion.

No matter where Buck traveled, the stories of his rope tricks traveled with him. In West Palm Beach, Buck swings a big loop over a crowd of dignitaries, including author George Plimpton.

Mr. & Mrs. Buck Brannaman at their wedding at the Cold Springs Ranch, with Betsy Shirley.

Buck and Mary on the big day with daughters Lauren and Kristin.

Buck holding daughter Reata.

Buck during an interview with ABC in Australia. Features on Buck's techniques were widely carried on television in that country.

During one of Buck's clinic trips to Australia he was asked if he had ever saddled anything other than a horse. This picture says it all.

Buck takes a break at his Sheridan, Wyoming, ranch during the filming of one of his instructional videos on roping.

Buck at a clinic in Eagle, Colorado, working with a young horse to untrack or "free up" his hindquarters. This maneuver helps the horse understand turning when asked by the rider.

The moment of "hooking on," when horse and man connect. Here the horse chooses to come closer to Buck as Buck moves away. It is as if they are linked by an invisible thread.

A horse's first ride is about establishing comfort with the rider's presence and about direction. Here Buck asks the horse to turn by moving away from his lariat.

Buck's mission is giving horses the best possible start in life. Here he visits with a mare and foal on his ranch.

Buck introduces Robert Redford to the correct use of the flag and to Rambo, Buck's new horse who would ultimately play Redford's horse "Rimrock" in the film The Horse Whisperer.

hind her driver, and I thought that was the way to travel. I can't see putting $250,000 into a car, but it was a nice ride, there's no doubt about it.

The polo grounds occupied the biggest flat spot—no trees or water—that I saw the whole time I was in Florida. There must have been a couple hundred acres of nothing but beautiful green grass and polo field after polo field. Everyone stared at me as I walked onto the grounds in my cowboy hat and boots. I felt like a bug in a jar.

A day or two later I checked out Royal Palm Polo at Boca Raton. A bunch of people were standing around a big chalkboard, and I figured they were signing up for some polo. So I promptly signed up. They were going to be playing that coming Sunday, and I thought if I wanted to get into it, the only way to do it was to show up.

I arrived early Sunday morning with my horses. Brett Kiley, a really good polo player from Perth, Australia, and manager of Jorie's horse operation in Florida, helped me braid their tails and get them ready. I didn't know anything about doing the polo braid, a knot that keeps the tail from getting tangled with the player's mallet, but with Brett's help I got them ready.

Someone came by with an armload of polo jerseys. When he saw what I was doing, he tossed me one with a number 2 on it. I had played enough organized sports, so I thought I'd just watch a polo match that was in progress; in that way I'd figure out what a number 2 does.

In the box seat that Jorie had reserved for me, I sat watching polo and eating onion sandwiches with other spectators. They were dressed in furs and dripping with gold and diamonds; I thought it was pretty funny that people who could eat anything they wanted to eat were eating onion sandwiches.

As the players galloped up and down the field, I discovered that you could take your opponent out of a play by getting your horse to push his horse away from the ball (I later learned that's called "riding off" an opponent). Although I didn't know a hell of a lot about offense, it looked to me as if I could handle that kind of defense. My horses were very comfortable being around other horses, and they could move up close to them. Thanks to all the ranch work they had done, especially roping other horses, bumping another player's horse off the ball seemed like a piece of cake.

As I was saddling up for my match, the man who ran the club came up to me. "Son, I can't let you play your horses in a plain snaffle bit. You're going to get somebody hurt, or get somebody killed."

Polo ponies are played in gag snaffles, full bridles with long curbs, and other severe bits that create the kind of stopping power the players want their horses to have. However, that wasn't my way. My horses were all capable of doing the quick turns and hard stops that ranch horses have in common with polo ponies, but mine went in plain snaffles.

So I replied, "I know that grounds fees for this club are seventy-five hundred bucks for the three months I'm supposed to be here. Why don't you just let me play a chukker or two, and if you think I'm dangerous to people, then I won't come back anymore. I'll just go back to Montana where I belong, and you can keep the seventy-five hundred bucks, and I'm out of here."

The fellow agreed that was a good deal, so when the time for my match came, I got up on my horse and went out on the field. During the first two chukkers, all I did was gallop up to my equivalent position on the other team and ride him off the ball. Every time he'd make a run for it, I'd ride up beside him and just shove him off. It seemed to work well, so well that I sensed a little irritation from him.

After a few chukkers and changing horses a few times, I started to pick up the rhythm of the game and how it was played, so I figured I'd take a swing if the opportunity arose. My chance came, and darned if I didn't score a couple of goals. This, my friends, was Montana luck. I could hardly hit the ball, but my horses turned around well and ran straight so I could line up my shots. That gave me a little more time to figure out how to time the swing with my mallet. I'd seem to end up in the right place at the right time, and I could smack the ball a few feet or more and get it to go between the goalposts.

I felt pretty good after the match. I hadn't cost my team anything, and, as my horses worked well, I hadn't embarrassed myself. Then the club manager came up to apologize. "I'm sorry to have doubted you," he said, "but you have to understand the type of horsemen or would-be horsemen that I'm used to seeing. You can play in a snaffle bit around me anytime." That manager's name was Buzz Welker, and we got to be great friends that winter. He's a very well-respected instructor who has taught polo out near Jackson Hole, Wyoming. I've seen him now and again.

Back at my horse trailer, an older fellow in a straw hat came up to me and asked, "What club did you play for all summer long, son?" A lot of players played in New York or in other northern parts of the United States in the summer season.

"Club?" I said. "Well, sir, I didn't play for any club. This was my first time."

"You mean here?" he asked.

"No sir, playing polo."

Because of my horses, he didn't believe me. Nobody did. Everybody thought I'd been in polo for a while. Thank goodness I didn't have to hit the ball very often to show them how inexperienced I really was. It was the defense that impressed them, I guess, and if it hadn't been for my horses, I probably would have embarrassed myself. Riding that fast swinging a hardwood mallet sort of sets you up for a mishap. My horses really carried me through.

That's the beauty of the foundation I put on all the horses that I start. The basics are all there, so you can then finish up a horse to do anything you want him to do, whether it's ranch work or horse showing or polo.

When I wasn't playing, I worked with troubled polo ponies, including a whole barn full that had been trashed by some of the pros. A lot of pro polo players had the hands of a butcher. They'd whip a horse on the butt to get him going thirty miles an hour to catch up to the ball, and about the time a player on the other team hit a back shot, they'd tear their horses' heads off to get them stopped and turned around and off in another direction. The horses were damned if they did and damned if they didn't. It was very frustrating for them, and it didn't take too long before their minds were blown.

Not all of the players were that rough, but there sure were an awful lot of them, at least in those days (nowadays, a shortage of good polo horses has placed a greater emphasis on better horsemanship).

Using patience, kindness, and consistency, I was able to get the horses to recover fairly quickly, to the point that they were able to play for me. As a result, I had some real top-notch polo ponies for the weekend matches. I didn't really do anything different with them than I'd do with any other horse, no matter whether it was troubled or just hadn't been started. I ride every horse pretty much the same way. Some of my cues may be a little less forceful with a horse that's been troubled and perhaps a little more assertive with one that's been spoiled. I ride the way I ride, and eventually all horses I've been on begin to look like my horses.

If I hadn't been around to work with those polo horses, they might have been sold to some local players at bargain prices. The locals wouldn't have gotten along with them either, and they'd have been sold again. Many would have ended up on a Frenchman's dinner table, some with sauce and some without.

The work I did might have convinced some people about my methods, but it didn't really change the way high-roller players treated their horses. They were too into their own thing. In those days, polo was all about money and winning punch bowls at tournaments.

Some great polo horses have come off ranches in the West. Some receive basic training at polo facilities in the East. These generally don't turn out very well because they haven't been exposed to the real world of moving cows and riding out in the hills. Being raised and trained in the East can be a pretty stressful experience for a horse.

My winter in Palm Beach was nice and warm, but it was also pretty expensive. Toward the end of my run there, I had my truck stolen right out of the hotel parking lot. I went to Texas to pick up a new one, and I drove it back, but before I packed my gear and headed for Montana, I had one more gig to do at the grand opening of the Vero Beach Polo Club.

Jorie, who had seen my trick roping, thought that it would be a wonderful thing as a part of the entertainment for me to demonstrate the way I trained a polo horse and then do a few rope tricks.

Prince Charles, who was a friend of Jorie and Jeffrey, had been invited to Florida to play polo at the new facility. When I got back from Texas, Jorie said, "Since you're going to do a training demonstration and then a few rope tricks, why don't you do a polo demonstration as well?" As it turned out, she had already set it up for me to smack some balls around with Brett Kiley.

That stopped me a little short. "Jorie, I don't feel comfortable hitting those polo balls around," I told her. Prince Charles was going to be there, and she wanted me to hit balls in front of him. Not only was he the future king of England, he was also a very accomplished polo player in his own right.

Jorie saw me start to sweat and said, "Dahling."—she always called me "dahling"—"you'll just take turns. You will hit one shot, and Brett will hit the other." I must not

During polo season in West Palm Beach the days and nights could get rather "western," as they say, and two guys from Montana—here Buck and his friend Greg Eliel—may need an eye-opener of coffee on occasion.

have looked convinced because she went on, "It'll be great, dahling, don't worry. Everything will be fine, you just trust me."

For the next couple of weeks, I was beside myself. Since Prince Charles was playing, there were going to be five or six thousand people watching, maybe more. That's a big crowd in any man's league.

Jorie and Jeffrey owned two or three hundred acres in Lake Worth, near West Palm Beach. The property included a private polo field, where all I did for eight or ten hours a day was ride horses and practice hitting. A couple of other guys rode on the grounds, but I was on my own.

When the fateful day came, the training demonstration was right up my alley, and that part of the program was all net, no rim. The rope tricks went well, too; I'd been doing them since I was a kid, so that was a slam dunk. Then came the polo demonstration.

Brett and I rode out to face a sizable sea of humanity, and the announcer started talking about polo. As he described the different shots we'd attempt, I loped up to my first ball, worried to death I'd top it. If I did, the ball would go about six inches, and five thousand people, including Prince Charles, heir to the throne, would be laughing at me.

I loped up, swung my mallet, and when I hit the ball, the sound was the same as a perfectly hit baseball. What's more, the ball soared about 125 yards through the air. Cool, I thought, but I also thought, What blind luck! I hope I don't have to hit another one . . . maybe I'll just let Brett go ahead and hit the rest.

But Brett hit a ball, then looked over at me, backed his horse up, and sort of pointed to the balls as an invitation to go again.

Off we went. We went through all the polo shots: neck shots and tail shots, forehands and backhands, from the near side and the off side. I don't know how it happened, I still can't explain it, but every shot I took, I hit the ball like Willie Mays hit baseballs. I never missed a shot. It worked out great, but I still couldn't wait for the whole thing to be over with.

That was a lucky day in more ways than one. I met some wonderful people, including Prince Charles. Considering my humble beginnings, I never imagined that one day I'd get to shake hands with a prince, and I was grateful for the opportunity. I also met George Plimpton, who's made a career of being "someone else" and then writing a book about it. So I felt a kindred spirit, since I was impersonating a polo player.

I don't know if I'll ever go back to Palm Beach for another polo season, but I met some good folks that winter, and I learned a lot about polo ponies. The experience made me a better hand with horses, and I know it made me a better teacher in terms of being a little more well rounded.

On the downside, I did see an awful lot of troubled horses. But that was one reason I was there: to help fix some of the horses. I saw a lot that wouldn't have had so many problems if they'd had better handling. And as for those masters with a polo mallet, some could handle a polo ball like nothing you've ever seen, but if you hanged them for being horsemen, you'd be hanging innocent men.

That's true of a lot of other horse events. The horse kind of takes a backseat to the event itself. The horse becomes the vehicle. So maybe that's the reason there'll always be somewhere for me to go. Those horses need someone on their side.

As long as I live and can swing a leg over, the horse has a friend who'll fight for him.

9
Farther Along
the Road

WE HAD TAKEN TWO TRUCKS full of horses down to Florida that winter, and we laid over in Baton Rouge for a few days' rest. While we were there, someone arranged for me to do a free demonstration to drum up interest in clinics in that part of the country.

Angel Benton, a friend from Colorado, asked a local trainer who was in the gaited horse business to find a horse for me to work with. I guess the fellow was insecure about a stranger from out of town coming in to show how to work with horses. He must have thought, This'll be good, and he lined up a horse.

He also didn't keep it a secret. "Hell of a crowd, for people who don't know me," I said to myself when I showed up.

A gray horse waited in the round corral. Before I went in, a Cajun man took me aside said, "I don't know you, Mr. Buck, but you watch that sum-bitch because I know him." No one else volunteered a thing.

© Ted Wood

A never-before-saddled colt at the Denver Stock Show, bucking wildly after Buck saddles him. Buck allows the horse to buck and run, getting used to the saddle.

I asked what had been done with the horse. When I do that, I'm not fishing for information about the horse. I'm interested in finding out about the person or people who've been working with the animal. That's because a horse's behavior reveals as much about a person as it does about the horse. Then, too, if my well-being depended on the accuracy in reporting a horse's background, whether intentionally or inadvertently, I'd have been dead a long time ago.

I was told the horse's owners had tried to start him a couple of times. He bucked off lots of people, and once, when he ended up with the saddle under his belly, he went through a few fences. That didn't surprise me. It happens all the time—it's as common as morning coffee.

© Ted Wood

Buck approaches the same colt in a gentle and friendly way after it finishes bucking.

As I started moving the horse around the corral, I asked myself, "This is supposed to be a two-hour demonstration?" Although I knew the fellow who found the horse thought it would take only a few minutes for the horse to eliminate me, I also knew I'd have the horse ridden in no time. Then what the heck was I going to do for the two hours?

The horse bucked pretty hard when the girth was tightened, but that was the extent of the excitement. So, to fill the rest of the two hours, I came up with every trick I could think of. I led the horse by one ear, by the lip, by his tongue. I even led him by his feet.

These things are based on the unspoken but very evident draw or appeal to which another creature responds. Please note that I say "creature" because the connection works for us humans, too. For example, you can ask another person to dance, but even though you say the right words, the way you say them may not attract him or her. On the other hand, the right "feel" can be sensed across a room without a word being spoken—think of the lyrics to "Some Enchanted Evening." The other person may have seen you and then made up his or her mind to dance the whole night with you even before you said a word.

And how do you know? You feel it. "Feel" is the spiritual part of a person's being. There are a thousand explanations for "feel," and they're all correct. Horses have it, and they use it all the time. You can't conceal anything from a horse: he'll respond to what's inside you—or he won't respond at all.

I ended up the demonstration by riding the gray horse all around and then swinging a rope around him. When I had finished, I stopped the horse, who stood there hip shot (meaning he was so relaxed, his hindquarters weight rested on one hip).

I looked around at the crowd. "I know a lot of you came here to see me fail, the way lots of people go to an auto race to see bad driving, not good driving. And then there's this boy here who lined up the horse for me." I called him a boy because he hadn't earned the right to be called a man. "The sad thing is he didn't know or care what would happen if I, a stranger to him, got hurt. Or worse. I might have a family to feed or a mother to support. All to try and prove a point that seemed important to him."

I turned to the guy. "I want to know what makes you so different from me. I say different because I can't imagine doing such a thing. Why did you do it to someone who *might* be a wonderful person, someone you might have liked knowing if only you got to know him? Just what is it that makes you so different?"

Of course the guy denied knowing anything about the horse—he was just getting me a horse.

I wasn't about to let the guy off so easy. "I'm not the only one here who knows you can't talk your way out of this," I said. "Now let me give you a piece of advice. You were sure this horse would eat my lunch. Well, you're a long way from where I live. Don't come out to my playground because we play a lot rougher out there. We have this sort of horse for breakfast. Heck, our kids have this sort for breakfast."

Later, as I was set to leave, I noticed three Cajuns standing off to one side and looking at me. I smiled and said hello, but they turned away. The fellow who had given me the warning saw what was going on. "Mr. Buck," he said, "those men don't want you to think they didn't appreciate what you did today, but they suspect you have the voodoo."

When I replied that I had no mojo—I was just a cowboy from Montana—the man laughed. "Well, they'll sure be happy to hear that!"

People want to know whether my approach works with other animals. It certainly does.

Hooking on with a dog is easier than with a horse. Dogs are predators, not prey. Dogs respond to food, while food training spoils a horse. It's seldom successful in the long run. The key to hooking on with a horse is to provide comfort. Comfort means more to a herd animal than it does to a predator.

Dogs are much more trainable than cats are. Characterizing cats is a lot like a husband observing his wife or a wife her husband: cats are gratifying, interesting, perplexing, frustrating, loving . . . all of these things and more. You control the destiny of a relationship with a cat the same way you control it with a spouse: peaceful coexistence.

When I worked at a ranch near Harrison, Montana, a cat showed up on my porch one day. He had pinkeye, so I doctored him with the pinkeye medication we used on cattle. The cat stuck around, and I named him Kalamazoo, after a Hoyt Axton song that was popular that year. For the want of something to do, I tried to see how much I could get done with Kalamazoo. I got him so he'd lead with a string around his neck, sit down, and roll over. He'd jump in the back of the truck. He always came when called. And I accomplished all of that without using food as a reward. Kalamazoo just had the capacity and the interest to learn.

Eventually, the coyotes got him.

Much can be learned from the nobility of horses, and from how genuine and pure their thoughts are. There is no reason for a horse to look at you any differently from how he would look at any other predator. But when he learns that the two of you can go together and that going with you is better than resisting and going in the opposite direction, a feeling of comfort settles in him. His frame of mind begins to change, and he begins to view you differently.

Sometimes you've done your groundwork and your horse is comfortable. You get on but you're tight, or worried. In that case, your body language is doing everything it can to get you bucked off, but your horse may remain settled even though you aren't doing much to help him. That's what I mean when I talk about the horse filling in for you. And filling in can be accomplished only after helping the horse gain a large amount of confidence before you step on.

Filling in comes from the horse's being comfortable and trusting, both of which come in turn from groundwork.

People often ask, "How much groundwork do I need to do?" The answer is, enough to keep your horse and yourself out of trouble; enough to keep yourself from getting bucked off and from getting yourself and your horse in a wreck.

In other words, the amount depends entirely on how much you have to offer the horse when you get on his back. If you're an experienced rider and can go with the motion without clashing with the horse's energy, the amount of groundwork is a lot less than if you haven't ridden much. If you're inexperienced, unsure, and fearful, you'll need to do a lot more.

Do people expect too much too soon? Most certainly. And a lot of times the people who expect too much too soon are the ones who are afraid. They want the horse to

"Always go back to the basics" is something Buck stresses. As with playing scales on the piano, allow the horse to warm up with you. Here Buck does a little reminder groundwork with Bif.

come through, to get over all the things that he's doing that frighten them without their putting in the time to help him. They want him to become advanced as soon as possible—if not sooner.

On the other hand, people who have realistic expectations and enjoy working with a horse, allowing him to come along at his own pace, are the people who are confident. These are the people who don't work with horses to stroke their own egos. They feel comfortable with the horse because they're comfortable with where they are now. And that helps them be comfortable with where they're headed.

People talk about horses that are lazy. That may be their opinion, but a lot of times I know it's something else. Having been through hard times myself, I know what it's like to be in a situation where you're basically a captive. That's where many of these so-called lazy horses are. They're captives doing time. As a kid, I couldn't go anywhere else physically, but mentally I didn't have to stay. Often the only way I could survive a really stressful situation was to go somewhere else in my mind.

Many people survive just that way when they're young, and I feel sure that horses do, too, a lot of the time. They can't open a gate, hitch up the trailer, load themselves, start the truck, and drive off. Physically they're captives, and they have no choice but to remain. Because of a stressful life, an unhappy life with a human, those horses have to go away somehow. They have to leave in order to survive.

When horses do go somewhere else, their response may be very aloof. Humans will think that they're lazy or that they don't care, that they lack desire. These horses do not lack desire. They have lots of desire, but their desires can't be fulfilled because they're living in the wrong place at the wrong time.

Therefore, I'll tell people who ask me whether their horse is being dull or listless or lethargic that the horse may have had to go away mentally to preserve the one and only thing that means anything to him. That's his state of mind, his well-being. It isn't always the case, but I've seen it happen quite a bit.

I don't know that there is such a thing as a bad horse, but some are certainly more difficult to work with than others.

It isn't always the fault of the owner. Sometimes, the owner has the best of intentions but lacks the knowledge, the ability, or the means to work with a horse that is in trouble. Horses just want to survive, and it can be hard for them to fit into the world we have created for them.

Some horses are so easy to work with that we refer to them as "born broke." These horses are open to just about anything we want to do with them. However, others aren't real inclined to get along with us. Some of them are so afraid of losing their lives that they are very difficult to work with. Either way, the responsibility lies with us. As horsemen, we have the ability to adjust to the needs of the horse as well as to his individual personality. We have what it takes to get along with him. Some people find a very troubled horse too much to deal with; selling him might be the best thing they could do.

Occasionally you will find a horse born with very limited possibilities. These are no different than children who are born retarded. Sometimes, a foal will get the placenta over his nose, become starved for oxygen, and then suffer brain damage before the mare can pull the placenta off. Or a horse is born with some sort of birth defect that makes it difficult or impossible to perform normally. With such horses, you try to do the best you can, and if they fall short of becoming great horses, you accept them for what they are and make the best of it. Horses can be only as good as they can be. The best thing you can do is wait until you know any horse before you begin to have expectations. Before

Some horses progress faster than others. Buck is able to lope this horse in the round pen on a loose rein.

that, you need a general knowledge of horses. And then you do the best you can with what you have to work with.

Punishing a troubled horse for what you determine to be bad behavior is punishing him for something that in *your* mind is wrong. But it isn't wrong in his mind. He's only trying to do what he believes he needs to do at the time. As a horseman, you should have the wisdom to see how the horse prepares himself and to understand what he has in mind.

Then, if what he has in mind isn't what you're looking for, you head him off. You redirect him. You change his mind. You change the subject, and you keep on changing it until after a while the negative behavior disappears.

I don't believe in waiting for a horse to do the wrong thing and then punishing him after the fact. You can't just say no to a horse. You have to redirect a negative behavior with a positive one, something that works for both of you. It's as though you're saying, "Instead of doing that, we can do this together."

When things start to go wrong with a child, there is nothing wrong with laying down some rules, with being strict and saying no. You can talk to a child, reason with him, but you still need to give him a choice. You need to give him someplace else to go in his mind, and something else to do so that he can succeed.

If you don't, if you wait for him to do the wrong thing because you weren't paying attention to your responsibilities and then you become angry and beat on him, he won't learn anything from what he did. He'll learn to fear you. He'll learn to be sneaky and covert about what he does. He may never learn to do the right thing. Instead, he is likely to learn nothing but how to fail.

Now, I'm not saying that everything is milk toast, fuzzy, and warm when you are working with a child or working with a horse. But at the point you become angry or you abandon your sense of reason and logic and become ruled by resentment and anger, by spite and greed and hate and all the other negative feelings that seem to run the world these days, you aren't going to be any more successful with your horse than you would be with your child.

Unlike a child, a horse makes it pretty convenient for you to live your life this way. You can say all kinds of things about him, and he is never going to step up to the microphone and say, "Hey, world, let me tell you about this human. Let me tell you what he's made of." But a horse will still make his feelings known, and if you have mistreated him because of your inadequacies, his behavior will tell on you. You may meet someone like me who will tell you what the truth of his behavior means. You may not enjoy hearing it, but the truth doesn't go away.

You can tell a lot about an owner's character by observing the behavior of the horse. Some people come to a clinic to become a little safer on their horses because they're scared or worried. Maybe their horses are scared and worried, too. Overcoming such problems is easy to accomplish over a period of days. I can help people become more confident and understand their horses a little better.

Quite often I've had people come to my clinics who are too passive. They don't assert themselves in ways that evoke respect from other people or from their horses. Because these owners behave like victims, their horses may have bitten them or responded in other disrespectful ways that reflect an owner's overly passive nature.

Many such people come to my clinics because, consciously or not, they're searching for a sense of strength that they haven't found elsewhere. A woman may have been pushed around or bullied by her husband or her kids as well as by her horse. Learning a little bit of horsemanship—learning how to take charge, set a goal with the horse, and then achieve it—can be a very liberating experience. It can have a positive influence and permeate the rest of her life.

Women often acquire a new perspective toward their lives and a new self-confidence during my clinics. They reassess their lives and relationships, and they often "clean house" when their husbands or boyfriends don't measure up or adapt to their new approach to life.

Other people are overly aggressive. I've had men who are too embarrassed to treat their horses in public the way they treat them at home. But their horses won't cover for them. Whatever the owner is like with the horse at home becomes apparent at the clinic, because the horse will behave in a way that reflects the treatment he's used to receiving. That's what I mean when I talk about a horse's honesty. And thank goodness they are that way—they would be difficult animals to work with if they were liars on top of being so athletic.

Many times people have told me that what they've learned from me about understanding their horses has helped them begin to understand themselves a little bit better and then allowed them to make changes that improved their lives far better than they could have ever imagined.

One such person was a chariot racer who lived near Big Horn, Wyoming. Chariot racing is a winter sport, and it has a following in some parts of the West. It's a lot like what

Charlton Heston did in the movie *Ben Hur*, except the chariots aren't usually quite as fancy and the horses that pull them tend to be about half broke. Some of the horses have never even been taught to drive. The racers harness them up, beat them over the rump, and away they go over frozen ground or through snowfields.

When the man from near Big Horn tried to harness a horse and teach it to drive, they got into a fight. The man lost his temper and beat the horse with a two-by-four until the horse was unconscious. Somebody called a veterinarian, but it was too late. The horse was still unconscious. He wasn't dead, but there wasn't anything the vet could do, so he had to put the horse to sleep.

Someone called the sheriff, and the man ended up in front of a Sheridan County judge. The charge was animal abuse, and the vet, a Dr. Wilson, was one of the witnesses against him. After the judge heard the case, he asked the vet what he thought an appropriate punishment might be. The vet suggested ordering the man to pay to take one of his other young horses to one of my clinics. He t--hought that teaching the man how to properly start a colt might help him learn something about understanding horses, an education that would be more effective than simply hitting him with a big fine. The judge agreed.

I hadn't yet moved to Wyoming from Montana, but I'd been giving clinics in the Sheridan area for a while, and the person who organized my clinic there told me about the chariot racer's offense and the judge's sentence.

On the one hand, I wanted to hate the man for what he had done to my friend, the horse. But after considering the situation, I realized that the man most likely expected me to hate him. He had probably hardened himself to what was coming, and he was mentally prepared to get through whatever hostility he might experience.

When the man showed up at the clinic, I treated him no different than any other student. Giving him the benefit of the doubt, I acted as though he'd done nothing wrong. The locals knew, of course. There was a lot of whispering about who he was and the horrible thing that he had done, so you can imagine the shame and regret the man must have felt.

I was the only person there who treated him well, and after a day or two he started to make progress. He started asking questions, and by the time the clinic was over, he and his colt were doing pretty well.

After everybody else had said their good-byes, the man stood off by himself near the corrals. I was loading my trailer when he came over. He was a big man, over six feet tall, and weighing about 225 pounds. He just stood there for a while.

I waited until he spoke. "I don't know what to say," he began. "This weekend has changed my life, and in more ways than you will ever know." With that he started to cry.

I gave him a hug. "I may never see you again," I told him, "but I hope what you've learned helps carry you through times when it's hard to control your emotions. I hope you find the wisdom you need to fix some of the things that aren't okay in your life."

He nodded, then shook my hand. "Well, thanks for giving me a start."

Dr. Wilson was a wise man. So was the judge. Making that defendant attend one of my clinics turned out to be as good a punishment as could have been dished out. He went through a few life-altering days, which also validated something for me, too. My initial inclination had been to be mean and vengeful because of what the man had done to the horse. Yet if I had, if I had approached him as an enemy, I wouldn't have accomplished anything. There would have been no chance for him to learn a better way.

To have been able to play even a small part in helping someone change his life simply because he's been to a Buck Brannaman clinic is a very humbling experience. I'm grateful for the opportunity. It is a real blessing, and when people lean on me for emotional and psychological support, I take the responsibility seriously. I do the best I can to help them along because we're all trying to figure out how to live our lives, how to get by, and how to answer a few simple questions. We're all involved in the same search. Horses, like people, should be treated how you want them to be, not how they are.

There are so many variables in a clinic that I can't control: where the horses are coming from; whether they're scared, upset, or otherwise bothered. Nor do I have control over where the students are coming from or whether or not they're going to be able to help the horses when they need help. I can tell students what they need to do, but I can't do it for them, and there's always an underlying worry that someone will get hurt or even killed (I can laugh now about Polack and the water jug, but it wasn't very funny at the time). A person can fall off a horse as easily as he can fall out of the back of a pickup truck or even stumble on the way to the bathroom and bump his head on the sink.

We all know that there's a chance you can lose your life doing some of these things. But a person's dying at one of my clinics, even if only due to sheer accident—the sort of thing that can happen to anybody, anywhere, anytime— could negate every bit of good I've ever done, no matter how many people I've helped or how many horses I've saved from the slaughterhouse. It doesn't seem fair, but it could happen. I always live in fear of something like that, and I just have to leave it up to the good Lord to help my students and me through.

In a clinic in Boulder, Colorado, I had about twenty people in the colt class. All but one of them were doing their groundwork, helping their horses get comfortable and readying them to be approached and handled. The man who wasn't doing the work owned a little paint colt that he'd tried to have started before. He had hired a local horse trainer who had failed. The colt was afraid of the trainer, and she was afraid of him.

Once Buck gets a saddle on a young clinic horse he goes through all the same actions he had previously done with the horse un-saddled. This is to reinforce that the horse has nothing to fear after the saddle is cinched up.

The clinic began with groundwork to establish the essential connections between horses and their owners. This owner, however, didn't participate in this phase. When I asked him why he wasn't working with his horse, he replied, "I've had enough of this bullshit. I'm ready to get on this colt and ride."

I was more than a little shocked at the answer. "Well, sir," I said, "these other people are trying to get their horses comfortable enough to where they can get on them. I can't make you do this groundwork, but your horse is a little bothered. I'd think you'd want to be working at having a little better relationship with him than you do. But even if you don't, you'll have to be patient because we aren't ready to get on the colts yet."

People who overheard the man couldn't believe that he wasn't more interested in working with his colt, since he had paid good money to do just that.

An hour and a half later, students were getting on their horses for the first time in the round pen and getting along fine. The man in question was one of the last ones to get on. I held on to his lead rope from the back of my saddle horse, and I asked him to make sure his cinch was tight. He said it was. Because he was a big man, I then asked him to get on about halfway, nice and smooth, but he still wasn't following my directions. He stepped up and got on almost halfway when the saddle slipped. It turned under the horse's belly, and he had to step off.

The turning saddle had pinched the little paint's withers. It scared him a little, but the horse recovered and still tried his best.

The man tightened his cinch, got his horse reorganized, and made another attempt to get on. He put his left foot in the stirrup, leaned over the back of his horse, grabbed him by the mane as I'd told him to do, and swung up. He had some trouble fishing around for his right stirrup, but he finally got his foot in.

Now he was sitting on his horse. At this point I asked him to do what I had asked the others to do: reach forward and rub his horse's neck, the same way its mother had nuzzled or licked him when the little paint was a foal.

Once again the man didn't follow directions. Instead of trying to soothe the horse, he reached up and slapped him on the neck in a very macho way. The sudden impact startled the horse, who moved his hindquarters six or eight feet to the left. The man's balance was so poor, he fell off. There was a snapping sound, and the man grabbed his leg up high by the hip.

Everybody got off their horses and led them out of the corral. While we were waiting for the ambulance, the man kept saying, "I'm sure sorry. I messed up the clinic for everybody, and it's not anybody's fault. It's my own fault. And I'm sorry. I'm sorry."

"It's all right," I told him. "Don't worry about it. We'll get you off to the hospital and get you fixed up."

The ambulance came and took the man off to the hospital. I asked someone else to ride his horse, and before the clinic was over, the little paint was taking part in my advanced horsemanship class, loping around out in the pasture and getting along just fine.

I was really proud of the horse, and I thought his owner would be happy that he had continued. The man had broken his leg, and when I checked on him a few times in the hospital, I reported on his horse's progress, wished him well, and told him I was sorry he'd had bad luck. And that, I thought, was the end of the story. I left town and went on to the next clinic.

About a year later, I was doing another clinic in the same arena when a kid in a T-shirt walked in. He didn't look as if he fit in at a horsemanship clinic, and he didn't. He was a process server. Right there in the middle of my clinic he served me with papers saying that my clinic's sponsor and I were being sued for wanton and willful negligence. The little paint's owner had accused us of having tried to get him hurt or killed, and that our intentions had been premeditated. He wanted a million dollars.

Nothing like that had ever happened to me. How could the man sue me for something I tried so hard to prevent? I was so upset that I just wanted to cry right then and there in front of everyone.

I had no insurance to cover such a matter, and I ended up spending thousands of dollars—that I didn't have—for an attorney I shouldn't have needed to defend myself from something over which I had no control.

The legal wrangling went on for the next couple of years. Over the course of the lawsuit, the million-dollar claim that the man had been after was reduced to ten thousand; his lawyer was looking for an out-of-court settlement to get his client something so the lawyer could make something for himself.

The night before we were to go to trial, my lawyer called. "If you give this man one of your custom-made saddles, he'll drop the case."

I was outraged. "You tell him that if he wants one dollar to settle out of court, he can go to hell." I had my principles, even if I was going to spend the rest of my life paying for them. I knew that the horse hadn't done anything wrong, and I hadn't done anything wrong. The only thing that got that man was gravity.

I was staying with friends in Boulder during the lawsuit. As I was about to leave for court the next morning, I received a call from a funeral home in Arizona. My father had died. The funeral director had been trying to get ahold of me for several days. He wanted me to sign a release allowing my dad to be cremated. He also said that the memorial service was to be held that day.

I called Smokie with the news. He was living on Michigan's Upper Peninsula, and even if he had wanted to attend the service, he couldn't have gotten there in time.

That day marked the end of all my hard feelings and memories of torment. I would very much have liked to have been at his service to say good-bye, but I couldn't go. I had to be in court.

While I was on the witness stand and the opposing lawyer was asking me questions, I broke down and began to cry. "What's wrong?" the lawyer wanted to know. He couldn't understand why his questions had provoked so much emotion.

"What's wrong is that I'm sitting here in court defending myself from something that even you know that I had no control over. I'm sitting in this court, wasting my time, when I could be at my own father's funeral." I looked at the judge and then the jury. "Instead, all of you are getting my time today because if I didn't show up for something like this, by default you'd give this sue-happy man and his lawyer everything I have ever worked for and everything I will ever work for. This is a choice I had to make today. It's a hard day for me."

The jury found on my behalf and awarded the man nothing. They agreed there was no fault on my part. The man had simply lost his balance and fallen off his horse.

Dad owned a little piece of property in Chino Valley, Arizona. He had some furniture that he'd made as a young man, as well as family pictures and a few of his great-grandfather's guns that had been passed down through his family. None of it was worth a lot of money, but he'd intended to leave them to me. A few days before he died, Lillian, the woman he had been living with, got him to change his will. I don't know if they were married or not, but she was his companion and had been looking after him. As a result of Dad's changing his will, all I inherited was a handful of pictures of my mother. Everything else was gone. Smokie and I never got any of it.

I didn't hate my dad when he died. At some level, I loved him. I didn't love him as I loved Forrest. Forrest was my teacher; he was the man who raised me and prepared me for life. My dad was the one who showed me the kind of man I have worked hard not to become. In that sense, you could say I learned a lot from him as well.

10
Horse Problems and People Problems

I OFTEN MEET HORSES in my clinics that are socially bankrupt. They are inept at being around other horses. This problem sometimes goes back to their separation from their mothers; humans may not have offered them a replacement that they needed to become secure within themselves.

Quite often, however, the environment is responsible, an owner who has a small piece of property or buys a house in a subdivision, then decides to get a horse or two. An environment like this is completely artificial compared to where God put horses in the first place. Even if the horse in such a situation gets to be around one parent or brother or sister, he doesn't get to be around other horses in a herd environment.

Going to a clinic is the first time such sheltered animals are around other horses. They're not at all equipped to fit into the equine society. They'll either be scared to death and want to huddle in a corner or be aggressively warlike in their actions.

It's all because the owner hasn't allowed his horse to be in a natural environment when he's not riding or working with him. The owner thinks he's doing his horse a favor by putting him in a box stall lined with varnished oak, with polished brass door handles and pretty pictures on the stable wall. He thinks he's really pampering his horse, when to the horse it's no different than living in solitary confinement. In fact, prisoners are given more room and more exercise than these horses.

Owners who put their socially bankrupt horses into a clinic's herd environment often feel resentment because their horses don't fit in. This resentment is motivated by the horse's discomfort, which creates in the owners a fear of getting bucked off or of the horse running or jumping out from under them. They're afraid of getting kicked or of the horse kicking somebody else.

Such horses are lost, but they don't have to be. Support from the rider, the kind of support that works with a horse's mind and causes accurate movements that are stimulating to him, will make all the other social issues irrelevant. When you ask for these movements, when your idea becomes the horse's idea, your mind and your horse's mind can become one. You then build on the horse's pride in such a way that he feels more secure within himself. The end result is a horse that will fit better in a social environment with other horses.

Someone who has a horse with social problems can't just go out and buy a herd of horses, then throw him into it and think that everything is going to be fixed. The horse missed out on his formative years, and trying to re-create them won't work.

A child psychologist could easily draw a parallel between such a horse and a kid who wasn't raised right by his parents, one who missed out on formative experiences that should have occurred early on. A kid who's thrust into an antisocial environment and who starts hanging around a bunch of gangster punks—the type of people who are drawn together because they're social deviants—won't develop socially acceptable behavior.

A horse with the same kind of social problem isn't any different. As a rider, you must slowly and methodically show your horse what is appropriate. You also have to discourage what's inappropriate, not by making the inappropriate impossible, but by making it difficult so that the horse himself chooses appropriate behavior. You can't choose it for him; you can only make it difficult for him to make the wrong choices. If, however, you make it impossible for him to make the wrong choices, you're making war.

Socially bankrupt horses are a lot like kids who come home from school with report cards that say, "Doesn't play well with others." There are many reasons for this sort of behavior.

A horse can be frightened of other horses. He's been sheltered and thinks the whole world is out to get him.

Because he's afraid, another horse doesn't have to be overtly aggressive toward him. A quick move by another horse or even a rider passing by can be enough to send the frightened horse into a fearful response. That can be unsafe for anybody sitting on him: he may jump out from underneath the rider or run away. Then, too, the rider may be just as scared. His response may be just as fearful as that of the horse: the rider might jerk on the reins or clamp down with his legs. That will terrify the horse even more, which just perpetuates the problem.

Using a flag usually teaches an insecure horse to be confident. A flag is a stainless-steel antenna with a strip of colored plastic tied to the end of it. At first it can be pretty

© Ted Wood

Buck uses the "flag" to get this horse used to outside sensations. The flag acts as an extension of his arm, and keeps him safe if the horse decides to kick or strike.

scary, but if you get the horse used to it while you're on foot, you can gradually get him to the point that you can ride while you carry it.

Carry the flag up, like a tennis racquet, because if you carry it down like a crop, the flag might disappear into your horse's blind spot under his chin. Then he'll become startled when you raise your hand and the flag reappears.

You wave the flag to encourage other animals to move away from you. Your horse will perceive that when you're riding him and using that flag, he (actually you) is causing other horses that he thought were superior to move away. That will build his confidence fast. He may have spent his whole life yielding to other horses, but when he realizes that he can cause them to yield to him, you will see quite a change in how your horse feels about himself.

Kicking or biting are other inappropriate behaviors. They don't always happen because a horse is aggressive; many times a horse kicks or bites because he's frightened. Sometimes he just feels as if he's been backed into a corner and has nowhere to go.

Imagine a situation where you're buried up to your waist in sand and people are walking all around you. How insecure would you feel if you couldn't move your feet and people were stepping on your fingers and pushing, running into, and kicking you? If you can't move your feet to keep from getting hurt, how violent would you become from the waist up? By the same token, a horse whose feet aren't freed up when he doesn't feel comfortable moving them is likely to show a similar violent attitude toward other horses. Another horse or rider crowding his space makes him feel he needs to bite or kick. Such a horse is scared and bound up within himself because he can't or won't move his feet to get away from trouble.

Regarding a horse that is inclined to kick, after he's already lashed out at someone, he should not be punished. It's already too late. Nothing good will come of it, and besides, you shouldn't be punishing him in the first place. Instead, a good horseman will observe what's about to happen and act before the horse has acted aggressively. You should tip his head toward the person or horse he was about to kick and use your leg to ask him to move his hindquarters in another direction. Or you might ask him to speed up or slow down. You might simply pick up on both reins and ask him to "drop" (another term for "tuck") his chin so he gives to the bridle.

Think of it as "changing the subject" or redirecting the horse's mind. That takes timing and foresight. You have to plan ahead so that rather than seek revenge for the horse's misbehavior, you see his aggressive behavior shaping up and can then redirect it. You change his mind before he's acted and move him on to something else.

Whether riding a horse or working with a kid, there's no crime in saying no. But always saying no will take away all the horse's desire to try, and pretty soon the horse or the youngster will believe there's nothing he can do right. But saying no and immediately redirecting with "but instead you may do this" will head off inappropriate behavior. That's all I think about when I'm riding a young horse. Instead of punishing inappropriate behavior after the fact, I redirect him before it occurs. Redirection is where the "instead" part comes in. Redirecting a horse gives his mind something else to do and takes him down a different road from the one on which he was traveling.

You hear a lot of talk about mentoring these days. It doesn't have to be just talk. If we get to troubled kids early enough, we can impress things upon them not by being mean and threatening, but by providing discipline and guidance.

The same thing is true for troubled horses. If you extend the parameters too far because of sympathy, the horse won't have any boundaries, and you will end up spoiling him. An "abused horse" that has been "spoiled" with sympathy is one of the most difficult kinds to work with: when you try to correct him, you end up putting him back in the same frame of mind he was in when he was scared. You're damned if you do and damned if you don't, because a spoiled horse may require you to be physically firm. Yet the physical firmness will bring out the fear and the terror that tells him he is in danger of losing his life. Finding the correct amount of firmness depends on the specific horse and the problem, but finding that balance is essential.

It's your responsibility when you start working with a troubled horse to set specific behavioral boundaries. It is at this point in the horse's life that we humans have an opportunity to show just how evolved we are. We can help the horse focus on constructive tasks that ease his fears and show him that he's not alone in a world of predators. If we don't, if we do nothing but sympathize, we're allowing him to slip into another realm of trouble.

A horse that has made a positive change in his behavior needs an opportunity to "soak," to concentrate on and digest what he has learned. He needs his quiet time. Given this opportunity, his response will be better the next time you work with him. Otherwise, to present a horse with a new problem to solve before he's had time to soak up the old one forces him to disregard what's he just learned in order to concentrate on what's next. And if you throw too many tasks at a young horse too soon, you'll destroy his willingness to try.

The same theory holds for working with children. If you don't give a child enough time for a new idea to penetrate and to be committed to memory, if you throw too much at him, you'll overwhelm him and destroy his desire to try, too.

Choosing the right moment in time to let the horse soak is crucial to his development. But also remember that he will soak on the bad as well as the good. If you have been fighting with a horse because he wants to buck you off or run away and you become discouraged and turn him out to pasture, he'll soak on this bad experience. He'll build on it, so by the time you work with him again, he is likely to be a lot worse off than he was when you turned him out.

On the other hand, if you've done good things before you turn him out and he soaks on what is positive, he'll be a bet-

Buck works a group of clinic horses with a flag after they've been saddled, getting them used to the feeling of moving with saddles touching them and stirrups flying.

ter ride than he was before. The important thing is to make sure the last word you have with the horse is good for both of you.

If horses are going to survive in our world, someone must lay down rules and then be persevering and disciplined enough to follow through. The same is true for kids. As parents, we have a chance when our children are young to turn them into good citizens rather than wait for the government to raise them for us. Once the horse or the human has grown older, there's much more danger in working with them. You must be much more disciplined and sometimes more forceful in order to provoke them to a point where they're ready to change how they live.

It's a matter of timing and of patience. Although it may seem nothing is happening on the surface, there may yet be profound changes occurring down a little deeper. Waiting isn't bad.

For me, these principles are really about life, about living your life in a way that you're not making war with horses or with other people. It's about planning ahead, rather than looking back and doing something in a reactive way. You need to be proactive when you're working with young horses. If a horse is inclined to kick or bite, you need to understand where that behavior comes from, what it's about, and how to redirect it rather than just punishing him for doing something you think is wrong. The horse thinks he's right, or he wouldn't be doing what he's doing.

We're supposed to be the smart ones, but it's amazing how people put little thought into working with their horses. They don't understand that a horse reacts the way he does because to him it's a matter of life and death. I often tell people in my clinics that the whole class could get on their horses and take off running, bucking and bouncing off the fences. That chaos wouldn't influence the horse I'm sitting on because he and I have a good thing going on. He doesn't go anywhere without me, and I don't go anywhere without him. Other horses and riders have no influence on us because my horse is secure within himself.

Wouldn't it be nice if we could raise our kids with that sort of independence? As parents, that's really what we're looking for. You look at kids who get into gangs or hang around a bunch of punks who will lead them down the wrong path. If the kids had been better equipped mentally and psychologically before they got around the bad element, the bad element wouldn't have had a chance.

You can't blame many kids who end up in gangs, and you can't blame it all on the kids who lead them into temptation. If their parents had given them a better background, they never would have ended up in trouble. Working with young horses is the same deal. In a sense we're parents there, too. We have a responsibility to help the horses become comfortable in their lives and understand how to fit in.

Herdbound horses are insecure, too, but for different reasons. A herdbound horse is fine if you go where the group goes, but quite often if you try to take him away from his pals, he may buck you off, tip over on you, or jump sideways out from under you. That's the kind of behavior that can get you hurt.

The horse doesn't feel secure with you because he doesn't feel secure within himself. As the rider, you can help him to stand alone and be by himself. Horses are very social animals that are meant to be in a herd, yet if you increase his sense of security with himself, your horse will be fine away from the herd as long as he has you with him.

A herdbound horse may have been left in the paddock for so long that he doesn't want to leave home, or he may be so used to company that he doesn't want to leave other horses and riders on the trail.

To start working on the problem, I'll have a group of people on horseback in a big pasture. They'll just be standing in a small group with room enough for a horse to move between them. I'll then pick a goal for my herdbound horse: a spot under a shade tree at the end of the meadow or some distant corner. I might loosen my reins and put them up on my saddle horn, start asking the horse to move with my legs, and ride near the group. I don't steer him with my reins or try to direct him with my legs. I simply cause movement. What I'm doing is making what he thought was a good place to be—the herd—a little difficult for him. I want him to understand that being alone with me in the corner of the pasture or under the shade tree is where he'll find the most security and comfort.

Rather than force my idea to become his idea, I *allow* it to become his over a period of time by making it difficult for him to stay with the herd. We simply walk and trot with nothing abusive happening. I tell the horse through my actions, "If you want to stay here with your pals, that's okay with me. I have no problem with that, but the conditions I'm putting on your staying with them is that you have to be in motion. They might get to stand comfortably, but you have to be in motion."

After a few minutes the horse may make a small circle away from the herd. When he does, my body becomes one with him. I pet him and rub him and am as soothing as I can be. Be still, and he'll go a little way and come right back to the herd—the herd is like a magnet, and he'll be drawn back with more force than I've been able to exert riding him off by himself.

After a few more minutes of keeping him in motion and thus making the herd an uncomfortable place to be, his circle will become a little larger. On the way out away from the herd, I pet him and rub him and praise him. When the herd draws him back, I keep a constant energy flowing through him. I turn the energy up in volume as we get closer to the herd, and I turn it down as we get farther away. It's kind of like the "hotter-colder" game.

With a horse that has a light feel to your leg, you may need only to ride him with a little faster rhythm to encourage him to step out and be more alive. But typically, a herd-bound horse has a tendency to pay more attention to the other horses and what they're doing than to listen to you. He tunes you out, so you may have to keep a firm leg on him in order to initiate and then maintain his energy. Sometimes, you can tap him with the tail of your reins to get his "life up."

Once you get the horse to respond, don't allow him to stop moving at the wrong time. If you do, he'll perceive stopping as a reward. Be careful not to let the energy diminish until the horse is in a place where you want him to be mentally and physically; that is, somewhere away from the herd or the barn.

Over a period of time, the horse's circles grow larger and larger. At first, he may move a hundred yards from the herd and stop. When he's in the general vicinity of the goal I've chosen, I pet him and rub him. He may not yet be sitting under the tree I've chosen in the corner, but he's closer to it than he was a while ago. I'll sit there for a while and I'll rub him, and we'll take a little break.

Then I'll ask him to move his feet again with my legs. I don't care where he goes. Typically he'll turn around and hotfoot it right back to the herd, looking for that secure place. But again, as always, when he returns to the herd, I make it difficult for him to be there. Soon he starts looking again for that place where things were more peaceful, so he moves a little farther out away from the herd, maybe toward the place he was resting before or even a little beyond it. When he gets there, I'll let him rest again.

The horse will build on what we're doing because I'm allowing his mind to search. I'm allowing him to change, to make changes within himself, without treating change like a life-threatening emergency. Even a real problem horse doesn't need more than an hour or two before I can comfortably ride with my arms folded to the tree in the corner of the pasture. There we'll sit for long periods of time. I'll pet him and rub him, let him enjoy the shade, and we'll just be together.

When I ask him to move again, he may turn around and lope back to his pals, but when we get there and he tries to stop, I keep him working at moving. That reaffirms that being with the herd isn't as secure or as comfortable as he thought it was. He'll look for his "comfort" tree in the corner of the pasture.

At the end of the lesson, I'll know that I've finished when the horse sits under "our" tree for a few minutes. Then when I ask him to move his feet, he'll take a step or two and offer to stop again. At that point, my idea and the horse's idea are one and the same. I'll step off him, take my saddle off, and rub him down with my hands (hands are a lot better than a brush right then because of the physical touch from a human being). And then I'll lead him home, maybe the long way. I'll take him back to the house and put him up, maybe give him a bite of grain, and put him away for the day.

Over three or four days, I'll set this exercise up the same way. When we're in the herd, I'll fold my arms with my

© Ted Wood

Buck puts the first ride on a horse that an hour before had never been ridden.

reins looped over the horn and let the horse simply walk off with his ears forward, open to anywhere I'd like to ride him, knowing full well that the place he's going to be most comfortable is with me.

The same approach with your own horse will build confidence in him. You're apt to be safe: you won't be bucked off or have your horse tip over on top of you as he fights you to get back to his pals. You're allowing him to be with them, but you're simply making it a little difficult for him when he's there.

This is an approach in which nobody loses and everybody wins. Once you've fixed a herdbound horse, you can ride with other people and he'll be content, not because other horses are with him, but because you are. It's just you and your horse, and it doesn't get much better than that.

Herdbound horses that can't be taken away from a group, that are too insecure to live their own lives as individuals, can be dangerous. A lot of people have been hurt or killed on such horses. To try the hairy-chested horse-trainer approach—showing your horse who's boss by sticking a spur in him or jerking his head off or whipping him when he wants to be around other horses—won't work. Force and violence never do. All you'll do is destroy what was potentially going to be a friendship between you and your horse. Plus, you're likely to get hurt. The macho approach to problem solving is used in many areas of life, and it simply doesn't work. It doesn't work at all.

* * *

Barn-sour horses are a lot like herdbound horses. Several years ago I did a clinic at the Mountain Sky Guest Ranch south of Livingston, Montana. The owner told me that he had a horse that his wranglers couldn't get to leave the barn. The horse either wanted to stay around the barn or he wanted to stay around his pals in the barn—the owner wasn't sure which, but both choices seemed pretty attractive to the horse. The wranglers had whipped and spurred him and jerked his head around, but rather than leave the barn lot, the horse bucked his rider off, rubbed him off against a fence, or flipped over backward.

When the owner asked if I would help work with the horse, I led the horse out of the barn, closed the door, and set things up so that he could move out through the barn lot gate and down the road if he chose to leave. I then asked one of the wranglers to step on and start moving him at the walk and trot.

I had the wrangler rub the horse and work his legs to keep moving. The wrangler rode the horse in figure eights and circles, all within twenty or thirty feet of the barn. I told the wrangler, "Make sure the horse understands that he can hang out at the barn with his pals as long as he's willing to work at it. Don't make things miserable for him, but don't let him stop and rest."

As I had done with the herdbound horse in the pasture, we were making the wrong choice difficult for the horse. It wasn't long before things began to change. The horse's ears went forward, and after years of being obstinately barn-sour, and generally miserable in attitude and expression, he trotted right out of the barn lot, through the gate, and down the road.

After he'd gone a couple of hundred yards, I asked the wrangler to get off, rub him, and let him stand. I asked him to pull his saddle off, leave it beside the road, and walk the horse the long way home. I then told the owner that if his wranglers repeated this process for a few days, they could turn the horse's life around.

The horse was twenty-one years old. For most of his long life he had been trying to do the best he could with what he knew. No one had ever offered him the right deal or he would have taken it. It wasn't as though he wanted to misbehave; he just didn't know bad behavior from good. All he knew was what people had made easy for him to do. Now, after all those years, we were asking him to change. Imagine being sixty years old and discovering that everything you thought was right about your life was actually wrong and that you had to change your entire existence.

Change can be difficult for a horse if bad behavior has become a lifelong habit. Still, he can change. This is an important lesson for people to learn, especially since people have a much harder time changing their own behavior. For example, there was a mother-daughter combination taking part in a clinic in Agua Dulce, California. Their horses were herdbound because the mother and daughter couldn't stay away from each other. The mother was spending too much time trying to help her daughter when, in fact, she was getting in her daughter's way and keeping her from making progress.

The same mother and daughter then took part in a ten-day clinic at my ranch in Sheridan, Wyoming. They aren't quite as bound together as they were, but the problem remains. I'm still working on weaning the daughter off the mother. They say it takes only twenty-one days to wean the colt off the mare. I've spent about six months with the mother-daughter combination, and we make a little progress every day of the clinic.

Every time I work with a horse—or a person—that's troubled or scared, I think of how the problems and solutions relate to a human's life, including my own. There are so many lessons, but it's important to remember that they're not all hard lessons and they're not all unpleasant to learn.

11
Mary

AFTER ADRIAN AND I WERE DIVORCED, Jeff Griffith and I were good friends again. When I wasn't off doing clinics, we teamed up to ride a lot of colts, hunt gophers, and fish during the day. At night we spent a lot of time running around, going to bars, and chasing girls.

I didn't date anybody seriously, but I sure dated a lot. I suppose I was so afraid of having my life destroyed again by a bad relationship that I didn't go out with any woman for very long. I kept everything pretty casual. Even though what happened between Adrian and me wasn't my fault, I felt so much guilt and shame about having been divorced that I decided I was going to stay single.

I wasn't really living anywhere in particular at this time. I was on the road doing a lot of clinics, and when I was back in Montana, I more or less lived up Indian Creek at Jorie Butler's place. When I didn't have a clinic to do, I'd ride her thoroughbreds and hang out with Jeff.

There have been times in my life when my choices in women have been fairly superficial. It was unique in my experience to meet a woman who is as beautiful on the inside as she is on the outside. Luckily I met one (given my track record, it had to have been luck). Her name is Mary.

I was doing a clinic in Boulder, Colorado, in 1986 when Mary Bower and I first met. She was one of the students, and she was the most beautiful woman I had ever seen.

Mary had been a fashion model, and at the height of her career she signed with the Ford Agency in New York. Even though she was assured of a lucrative career, she didn't like the idea of living in New York City, and after a couple of weeks she left. She moved to Los Angeles, where she appeared in a lot of print ads and commercials. She had some bit parts in television shows, but after a while she moved back to Colorado.

At the time we met, Mary was married to a former Denver Broncos football player named Rob Swenson. They had two young daughters, Lauren and Kristin. Her marriage was in trouble, but she hadn't filed for divorce yet. Rob was living in Denver where he was trying to get a real estate business going, and she was in Boulder with the two girls.

I had had a policy of never dating my clinic students, but when I watched Mary lope circles on her colt, I decided if I were ever going to break that rule, I'd have to marry her. I loved her from the moment I first saw her. It may sound like a scene out of a Harlequin romance, but something told me that this was the woman I would spend the rest of my life with.

After Mary had been to a number of my clinics and we'd started getting to know each other better, I sent her a note. I told her how much I thought of her and how much our friendship meant to me. I also told Mary that I didn't want to take her money for the clinic because I knew how hard it was to come by. I found out years later that she had been mowing lawns to come to my clinics.

Buck and Mary.

Mary called me the night she received the note and thanked me. She told me that the note made her cry. Her marriage had been an unhappy one, she had two young girls, and she didn't know what to do.

I told her, "Mary, I want to be with you more than anyone else in the whole world."

We started spending hours together, talking and getting to know each other. Mary knew quite a bit about me even before we'd met because I had a public life. She'd heard about Adrian and some of the things I'd fought through, but as we got to know each other better and began to trust each other, I shared with her things about myself that I normally don't share with anybody. Because I spend a lot of time talking into a microphone, people assume that it's not easy to hurt my feelings. It is. I'm just as sensitive as the next person, but it's hard for people to see that in my line of work.

I didn't say anything about Mary to my friends in Montana yet, but I did tell my foster mom about her. I told Betsy how much it meant to me to know this person, and I asked her to pray for me that one day we would be together because Mary was the person I always wanted to be with.

The turning point in our relationship came when I put on a clinic at the Pass Creek Ranch outside Parkman, Wyoming.

The students and I were all staying at a little guest house on the ranch. One night I ran out of chewing tobacco (I still had that unsavory habit), and I was headed for the Parkman Bar on the border of the Crow Indian Reservation to buy some. Mary, who was there with her sister Mindy, said she wanted to ride along with me.

As soon as we got into the truck, Mary asked in her direct way, "So, Buck, what are we going to do about this?"

I blurted out, "You could spend the rest of your life with me, and then it wouldn't be a problem. I've loved you for a long time, Mary."

She looked at me for a moment, then she smiled and said, "Me, too."

It was all that needed to be said. I don't know if the Parkman Bar was five miles away or five hundred. The moment was forever.

After we got back to the ranch, we walked out to check on the horses. Until that point, we had never even held hands. But there in the Wyoming moonlight, with the world spinning around us, we held each other and kissed.

The divorce wasn't particularly friendly when it came, but it wasn't as bad as some. Even though I think Rob respected me, it was hard on him, and it was an adjustment for Kristin and Lauren. They were five and seven at the time, and at first they were confused that their mother wanted to be with me instead of their dad. She had always been a wonderful mother, and the girls knew she loved them, but it wasn't easy for them, either.

Mary came out to Montana once or twice a month and stayed with me at Indian Creek in the Madison Valley. We spent most of the rest of the time on the phone. Our phone bills were close to the national debt.

I proposed while we were sitting on a bridge over Indian Creek in Ennis, Montana, where I was doing a clinic. Mary was again direct. She asked, "What do you intend to do about this?" She meant our relationship.

I replied, "I intend to spend the rest of my life with you."

That is how it happened, on a summer evening on the Madison River, under a moonlit sky . . . the whole nine yards.

Mary introduced me to her girls over the July Fourth holiday in Jackson Hole. We rode the gondola up to the top of the Tetons—Kristin called it the gondelo. I felt strange at first, because I didn't know anything about children. All I knew was about being single, but we had a lot of fun.

I had met her parents, Bill and Lorraine Bower, in Boulder a few months after we started going out. Bill had been a fairly well-known aviator during World War II. He was one of Jimmy Doolittle's raiders flying B-25s, and he was part of the raid on Tokyo that was America's response to Pearl Harbor. We got along just fine.

Her close friends were all for us, and so were her brothers Bill and Jimmy. Mindy was excited that we were going to be brother and sister-in-law, but some of Mary's other friends probably thought she'd lost her mind. She was a beautiful model who had been around some fairly influential people. She knew just about everybody in Boulder, and here she was running off with a cowboy. I'm sure they were shocked, but Mary and I were so consumed with love for each other that, quite honestly, neither one of us gave a damn what anybody thought. If they couldn't accept what we had de-

Buck, center, with some of the women in his life. From left: Mary's sister Mindy Bower—a superb horsewoman—Mary's daughter Lauren, Mary holding daughter Reata, and Mary's daughter Kristin.

cided to do with our lives, then they weren't really our friends after all.

Mary and I were married July 6, 1992, in an outdoor ceremony at my foster parents' ranch. Mary's girls, her folks, and my foster mother, Betsy, were there, along with most of our closest friends. They had seen us go through some hard times, and they were thrilled for us. They seemed to feel we were getting the happy ending that we'd both been waiting for.

Kristin and Lauren were flower girls. Instead of having a specific best man and maid or matron of honor, we wanted all our friends and loved ones to play that part. Preacher Dave conducted the ceremony. As it turned out, we were the last couple he married. Not long after our wedding, he quit being a preacher and moved down to Oklahoma where he started selling mobile homes.

We lived around Bozeman for the first couple of years after we were married. We bought a house on five acres outside of town and kept several horses. I was busy doing clinics, and at first Mary found having me on the road as much as I was somewhat difficult. She's learned to handle it pretty well since, but maybe that's because a little bit of me goes a long way.

I began learning how to be a stepdad. Kids have a forgiveness for their real parents that they don't have for stepparents. That means there are two different playbooks, two different sets of rules. Kids are almost looking for you to become the wicked stepfather or stepmother. That validates situations so that kids will have a scapegoat, which gives them a license to misbehave.

My primary object was to become friends with Lauren and Kristin. That's how I learned that you pick your battles more carefully, and there are times you have to let go. Things have worked out well at our house: the girls are straight-A students and model citizens.

That goes back to what I've said: whether you're dealing with a kid or an adult or a horse, treat them the way you'd like them to be, not the way they are now.

I taught the girls to ride, and Mary and I rode with them some, but they never really got into horses. Their real passion has always been schoolwork, which is a full-time job. I'm really proud of them, and I love them as I do my own daughter, Reata.

Mary got pregnant in the summer of 1993, the year we acquired the Houlihan Ranch in December. We had looked at some other places, but Mary liked the country around Sheridan, Wyoming. We heard that the ranch was available when I was doing a clinic in North Carolina. The property was a thousand acres of grassland and rolling hills, and when I got a descriptive package from the Realtor handling the sale, it looked like a good deal. Worried that the ranch would be sold by the time I got back, I made an offer sight unseen. Buying property that way can be risky, but it turned out to be one of the best decisions I ever made.

The house was old, but we remodeled it according to our tastes. I built corrals and a lot of new fencing myself, and the work I did on *The Horse Whisperer* helped pay for an indoor arena so that I've got a place to ride in the winter. That makes a real difference when the snow is coming in sideways at seventy miles an hour.

Our newborn daughter was named Reata, which in Spanish means a rawhide rope "of great strength"; Mary and I loved the sound of the word. Reata was born on March 30, 1994. I was in Malibu, California, doing a clinic. I had arranged to take time off so I could be present when the baby came, but Mary delivered a week early, and I just couldn't get home fast enough. I'll be sorry for the rest of my life that I wasn't there to see her birth.

It's generally accepted that if you're in the pattern of being abused by one or both parents, that's what you're going to do when you grow up. I don't agree. I believe the deciding factor all boils down to free will. People have the choice. Self-discipline prevents that streak from coming out. You need to be vigilant to guard against a slow growth in the wrong direction. You need to be cognizant of how you behave toward your wife and children. Not a day goes by when you don't think about how you want to be and how you *don't* want to be. It's always in the back of your mind, a burden that you carry.

Mary runs the ranch when I'm on the road doing clinics. We keep approximately forty horses and, depending on the summer grass, we run anywhere from one hundred to six or seven hundred steers. We ship in the fall, and Mary can do it all. She's a good hand and resourceful, too. She takes care of the horses; she moves the cattle when it's time to change pastures; and when there's a tractor job that needs doing, she jumps on and does it. When I'm at home, we work together; but when I'm on the road, she's on her own. It's like the old saying goes: "You never want to have a bigger ranch than what your wife can run."

It's hard being on the road so much of the time. I miss my family a lot when I'm gone, and it seems unfair that I have to be away from them as often as I am. Mary and I remain absolutely committed to each other, but I have a calling. I have a mission, and I have to fulfill it.

12
Whisperings

THE TERM "HORSE WHISPERER" was first used in ancient Scotland, but since the novel and the movie, the phrase has been used to describe trainers who have developed methods of working respectfully and gently with horses. It defines what I do for a living. It's not a bad definition, but it's incomplete and somewhat misleading.

I observe the horse, learn from him, and remember the experience. Then I try to find a way to use what I've learned to fit in with what I'd like the horse to do. These are the techniques that I learned from men like Tom Dorrance, Ray Hunt, and others who were using them long before I ever did.

I can't say enough about Tom Dorrance and Ray Hunt. Tom is a genius. He has spent his entire life observing horses and learning from them. He knows them inside and out, and he loves them more than any man I have ever known. He's in his nineties now, and he remains as curious about the horse as he ever was. His curiosity and his search for perfection are the cornerstones of his wisdom. Ray Hunt, who has followed in Tom's footsteps, is, in my opinion, the greatest horseman alive.

In 1994, I learned that a writer by the name of Nicholas Evans in London was trying to get in touch with me. He was doing research for a fictional character in a novel who would be based on the concepts I use when working with horses. He had called friends of mine around the country; his phone messages followed me from clinic to clinic. They said that he'd heard about my horsemanship techniques, and he wanted a chance to meet me.

Nick also called my ranch and told Mary he was having a hard time getting me to call him back. Mary made a suggestion. "If you want to talk to Buck Brannaman, you ought to go to one of his clinics and spend some time with him. If he feels you're for real, he'll help you get the information you want."

Nick took her at her word. He flew out to Novato, California, where I was doing a clinic and spent a few days with me. He watched me work with horses and listened to me talk about my methods. He told me his interest was in formulating the essence of a fictional character who would eventually become Tom Booker in the novel.

Nick is a very nice guy, and I got along with him well. But I've been on the road for many years, and in that time I've had more smoke blown up my backside than you can imagine. Lots of people were "going to write a book." Nick said he was going to write a novel. I left it with, "Well, Nick, good luck to you. I hope I've been able to help you and that it all works out."

Nick took his notes, we said our farewells, and he went on his way.

The next thing I knew, *The Horse Whisperer* was selling about a zillion copies. For those of you who haven't read the book or seen the movie, *The Horse Whisperer* tells the story of a fourteen-year-old New York girl named Grace and her horse Pilgrim who are injured in a terrible riding accident. When Grace's high-powered mom, Annie, realizes that in order to help her daughter recover, she has to help Pilgrim, too, she gets in touch with Tom Booker, a cowboy and horseman who is famous for his ability to work with troubled horses. Tom lives on a ranch in Montana where Annie takes Grace and Pilgrim. After Tom begins making progress with Grace and Pilgrim, he is able to help Annie with her own problems as well.

Nick called me a few months after the book was published. This time he actually got ahold of me, which is no minor miracle when I'm on the road. He thanked me for all the help that I'd given him, and he told me he had sold the movie rights. After we had chatted for a while, I congratulated him on his success, and we wished each other the best. Again, I thought that was the end of it.

About a year later, in the spring of 1996, I was doing a clinic in Ojai, California. A young woman I'd seen at several of my California clinics introduced me to a fellow named

Patrick Markey. He had long hair, and he was wearing jeans and a pair of shoes that reminded me of the old earth shoes from the 1970s. I was a little surprised to learn he was a movie producer; I thought that all producers went around wearing suits. A lot I knew about Hollywood producers.

After we said our hellos, I excused myself and went over to the arena, where I'd seen a young filly had been kicking. I put a rope on one of her hind feet so I could work on her "giving." I'd pick her foot up and set it down, and she was gradually getting better.

"Tell us all about what you're doing there, Buck," the woman with Patrick said.

"Well, I'm just trying to get this horse a little better about her feet. She's kind of touchy, especially around her hind feet, and that can be kind of dangerous for both of us."

Patrick didn't look like a man who cared about horses, but he was really paying close attention. Then he came over during the lunch break and asked, "What do you think of *The Horse Whisperer?*"

I told him I liked it and that I was very happy for Nick Evans's success. Nick was a good guy and deserved it.

"What about the horse scenes in the book?" Patrick went on. "I mean, how did you feel Nick did in interpreting what you do?"

"Well, Nick wasn't really trying to teach people how to work with horses. That wasn't his intention. So you can't look at the book as instructional material." I thought the book was a love story with a main character who happened to be a horseman. I liked it because Nick had written some-thing that was a little different from what I typically read. "I can't criticize Nick for not being able to portray the action with the horses exactly." If someone wanted to hang Nick Evans for being a horseman, they'd be hanging another in-nocent man.

Patrick continued, "Well, what would you change about the horse scenes in the book?"

"If you want to know the truth, I'd start over."

He laughed, and said, "Would you be interested in giving us some advice on this movie?"

"Yeah, sure," I nodded, thinking that all the advice he would want would amount to a few short phone calls from a hotel room wherever I was giving a clinic at the time. We shook hands, and he went on his way.

Little did I know that the film was to be a Robert Red-ford production and it was already under way.

As they say in Hollywood: "Dissolve to."

A few weeks later I got another call from Patrick. He wanted to set up a meeting at Mr. Redford's offices in Santa Monica. I was still in California doing clinics, so this worked for me time-wise.

I told Bill Reynolds that Redford's people had contacted me about the movie and asked him if he would play agent for me. Bill is a businessman with a background in the ad-vertising and western apparel worlds, and he loves horses. After we'd gotten to know each other and become friends, he began sponsoring some of my clinics in California, and he also partnered with me on several horse-training video and book projects.

My concern, and Bill's, too, was that we get the horse scenes right so that they honored my way of life and what I do for a living. On that basis, we agreed that the movie could be a great opportunity.

Quite a few people were on hand for the meeting. Bill and I were there along with technical advisers for other areas of the film. The offices contained western sculpture, Navajo rugs, and overstuffed leather couches, the sort of furnishings you might see in a house in Santa Fe.

When an assistant took me into Robert Redford's office, he was on the phone, and when he got off, he said, "Hi, I'm Bob."

We talked some about horses and where we lived, and it turned out that we had some mutual friends. I knew Mike Shinderling, his ranch manager in Utah, and Tom and Meredith Brokaw had been friends of mine for many years and friends of his as well.

After we chatted for a bit, Bob asked, "So, Buck, what do you think of the script? Is there something you can help us with?"

I said, "Well, if I was going to be on the payroll, I'd kind of want to know if you want me to just help you re-create what's in the book, or if you really want to know what I think."

He smiled. "I want to know what you think."

"If you want to get it right for the people who know this approach to horses, I'd rewrite the horse scenes and start over."

My response surprised Bob a little bit, but he understood what I was saying. He is a stickler for accuracy, and he wants to know that what he's doing is real. *A River Runs Through It* was a graceful, elegant film in part because Bob didn't phony up the fly-fishing. He took the time to get it right.

One of his assistants came in to say, "Bob, it's time to have the others come in. I'll go get them."

Bob replied, "No, I'll get them." It wasn't a big thing at all, but I was impressed. He got up, went out into his waiting area, and greeted everybody individually. Bob Redford was just a real outgoing fellow, friendly, polite, and very respectful. There was some real quality to this man, something that he would show over and over in the coming months.

Several days after the meeting, Bill and I arranged for Bob to come out to Bill's place in Malibu to talk about the movie and also to do a little riding. Patrick and an assistant came with him. Bob and I spent time on horseback in Bill's round corral. We discussed a major scene in the film, the one in which Bob's character, Tom Booker, lays Grace's horse Pilgrim down, a technique many horsemen use with troubled horses to help them get through barriers. Done right, it isn't all that dramatic, but it can be a very rewarding and freeing moment for a horse that is bothered, fearful, or defensive.

Bob wanted to see what that looked like. I had a horse with me that I had "laid down" before. This horse was used to it, and he kind of enjoyed it when he knew he was in no danger.

During the preproduction work on Robert Redford's filming of The Horse Whisperer, *Buck was one of Robert Redford's doubles in the picture. Here he strikes a recognizable stance.*

I put a rope around one of the horse's front feet and half-hitched my end to the saddle horn. Then I drove the horse around the corral for a few steps and pulled on the horn. He laid right down.

Bob didn't think it was that dramatic either. "There's not much there, is there?" he said. "I thought it was going to be a lot more moving." He was expecting some resistance or at least a cloud of dust. But it wasn't like that at all. The technique isn't intended to be violent, and besides, the horse was at peace.

We talked the problem over, and we decided we could make people think lying down was more dramatic by adding sound effects, slow motion, and also by making the horse look sweaty, as though he was working harder than he was.

Bill, Bob, and I agreed that we were going to work together on this film. I was hired to serve as technical adviser and horse trainer and to work as Redford's double when necessary. Bill was also a technical adviser to provide liaison with the western print media world.

We worked on the script for the next year. Any change in a scene that involved livestock produced a ripple effect, so a lot of other things had to change as well, such as dialogue and the shot list (the order in which scenes were filmed).

A lot of dialogue didn't really fit. Hollywood cowboy talk wouldn't cut it, so Bill and I worked long and hard with the film's research people to create a realistic tone for the western characters who were part of Tom Booker's world. Between us, we contributed maybe fifty lines to different scenes in the movie, and Bill gave them a lot of advice about authentic wardrobe. He outfitted Bob in some fine silver buckles through the Bohlin Silver Company, which Bill owned at the time.

We worked on the film for all of 1997. Shooting started in May and wrapped up sometime in September, and in the middle was one of the wettest summers that Big Timber and McLeod, Montana, had seen in a long time.

The hours were long, but we had some great times. Mary and the girls got to hang out on location. Mary had met Bob some years before when he was making *The Electric*

Horseman and had liked him. The girls were a little in awe of the stars, and for the first time I think they were really proud of their stepdad. In any event, I had a chance to impress a couple of teenage girls, at least for a short while.

One of the most challenging scenes to create was the one where Tom Booker roped Pilgrim inside a round corral filled with other horses. The camera and sound crews were all squeezed together in the center of the corral, along with a million dollars' worth of equipment, and we were trying to keep the horses moving in a circle around them. We had a stunt horse who could really run as a double for Pilgrim. The point of the scene was that Bob, as Tom, was having trouble catching Pilgrim and decided to rope him, and a running horse looked more dramatic.

To add to the fun, Bob is left-handed. I'm not, and I had spent the better part of the summer roping left-handed so that I could double for him. Another fellow, stunt rider Cliff McLaughlin, had also been practicing, and between the two of us, we figured we could pull this scene off and make it look as if Bob roped the horse.

So there we were: crew, doubles, and equipment all crunched together in the middle of the round corral with a horse running around us. The shot required either Cliff or me to rope Pilgrim's double, but once we got the job done, we had to get that rope off him before he clotheslined everybody in the middle of the corral, not to mention wiping out all the equipment. The rope had a breakaway honda on it, so all we had to do was pull and it would slip right off.

Still, we had to rope the horse in the right place so the cameras got the shot, plus we had to keep from roping him and the fence at the same time.

Bob and I had been talking about this scene for a few days. Knowing how much he wanted to get things right, I asked if he had ever run up against something like this before.

He told me a story about an incident that occurred while filming his mystical baseball picture *The Natural.* The crew had been working on a shot that had the same linchpin quality as the roping shot we were setting up. That one came during the climactic scene in which Bob's character, Hobbs, comes to the plate with Wonder Boy, the bat that he'd made as a kid, and gets ready to hit the home run that wins the game.

Bob had hired a professional hitting instructor to work with him on his swing, but he'd gotten so busy with other aspects of making the picture that he hadn't had time to practice much. The idea was that he'd step up to the plate, swing at a couple of pitches on camera, and then have the professional hit the ball into the seats. The camera's cutting from the ball as it left the pitcher's hand to Bob and the bat and back to the ball as it set off the scoreboard fireworks would look like he had hit the home run.

The extras in the grandstands had been kept waiting for hours. They had been given popcorn, candy, and soda pop in an effort to keep them happy. The idea was when the pro stepped in and hit the ball, the crowd would stand up and cheer as though they were watching a real ballgame. But it had taken so long to get the shot set up, the assistant directors were about half worried that the extras were not going to respond as happy fans were supposed to.

Much to everyone's surprise, it wasn't the pro who came out to swing at the pitch. It was Bob. He looked around at the stands filled with people, and, he told me, he got caught up in the moment. He turned to his director of photography and asked, "Why don't I take a swing or two and see if I can hit the ball."

Well, who was going to tell him he couldn't take a pitch in his own movie?

Bob stepped up to the plate and son-of-a-buck if he didn't drill the ball into the seats. As you can imagine, the crowd of extras went crazy, the camera operator got the shot, and Bob was thrilled. Who wouldn't have been? Bob is a good athlete, but, as he also told me, that was Redford luck.

The day came when we were finally ready to shoot Pilgrim's double in the round corral. The plan was now for me to do the roping, since the crew already had film footage of me roping the horse from behind. The shot they now wanted was of Bob swinging a rope as the horse ran past him. He had been swinging pretty well, but nobody wanted him to actually throw a loop because everybody was afraid he'd wipe out all the equipment, not to mention the crew.

Just before the cameras were ready to roll, I leaned over to Bob and said, "Why don't you try to rope him. You got pretty lucky with that baseball movie. You might just pull this off."

Needless to say, everybody else was pretty nervous about this swell new idea of mine. They didn't want to see Bob or anybody else get hurt.

Bob just grinned and said, "Why not?"

As he swung the rope and we drove the horse around the corral, I coached him, "Keep swinging, keep swinging, keep swinging—throw!"

And damned if Bob's throw didn't catch the horse around the neck. The crew got the shot. Everybody went crazy, and Bob couldn't believe it either. He enjoyed the moment so much that he wanted to try it again. I did the best I could to dissuade him. "Why don't we just be grateful for what we've accomplished, and quit while we're ahead?"

Buck ropes off his big chestnut thoroughbred Pet. Pet has his own claim to stardom as he was one of the horses who played the "lead horse" in the film The Horse Whisperer.

He thought it over, and knowing that things had worked out as well as they possibly could have, he agreed.

Ironically, one of the most touching scenes we shot wasn't used in the movie at all.

It featured Grace and Pilgrim at a point in the story where the healing process was beginning. The script called for Grace to enter Pilgrim's stall. Pilgrim was supposed to still be afraid and worried around humans, so he was to back away from Grace, stop, and then slowly walk up to her. She was then to pet him on the forehead and take his head in her arms.

It was really a moving moment, but the horse that was playing Pilgrim that day was having a little concentration problem and wasn't performing as we wished.

It had been raining like crazy all day, the way it had all summer, and we'd been working inside for hours because of it. Even though the set was calm, people were frantic at the thousands of dollars a minute they were spending while everybody stood around toeing the dirt.

Three different horses were playing Pilgrim. One, named Pet, was mine. Some of his hair had been clipped and a kind of stain had been applied to his skin to make it look like scabs from his injuries. When I was asked if I had any ideas, I mentioned Pet, who had been standing around all day wearing his Pilgrim makeup.

The first assistant director, Joe Reidy, gulped. "How long's it going to take you to get him ready?"

I said, "Well, if I don't have ten or fifteen minutes, I probably can't get it accomplished."

He burst out laughing. "I was expecting you to say you needed three or four days or a week."

The way the scene had been written, Pilgrim didn't have anything on his head, not even a halter. I had to get the horse to move straight forward and straight back on a line called a mark so that when the cameras were set, his movements were in frame. This was fairly precise work. A few inches either way messed up the shot, and I had to get it done without a halter rope.

I put a rope around one of Pet's front feet and taught him to move back and forward one step at a time. After a few minutes, I could feed out the end of the rope and he would back straight down the alleyway in the barn. Then, with a little pressure on the rope, he came back to me again.

When I told Reidy I was ready, the crew came back in and we started to shoot the scene. The camera was on a set of narrow tracks so that it could be moved back and forth in the stall to follow Pilgrim's movements. I sat down between the tracks with the rope laid along the stall floor. Scarlett Johansson, the talented young actress who played Grace, moved into position, with the rope between her feet.

I asked Pet to move back, and he did. Then I jiggled the rope, and he pawed at the dirt as though showing aggression toward her. Finally, I asked him to move slowly toward her. Pet was a horse that truly did love people, and he had a good feel about them. I'd worked with him in a way that he felt a special bond with all humans, so he responded to Scarlett the same as he would have to me.

When I drew the rope in and asked him to lead forward, Pet came up to Scarlett and put his head right in her chest. Scarlett was so moved that she began to cry. So did I, and so did everybody on the crew. To watch that little girl put her arms around that horse's head and give him a hug and cuddle him was one of the most wonderful things any of us had ever seen. For a brief moment we weren't filming a movie or doing any other kind of business. We were watching a special moment between a young girl and her horse.

The scene was cut because it detracted from the impact of the end of the movie. Nonetheless, seeing a horse respond to a little girl was a timeless moment, one that happens at barns every day. There's something magical about a horse and a little girl, and that's a good story, no matter what.

Toward the end of the summer we got ready to shoot the scene in which Bob lays Pilgrim down. As his double, I was the one who was going to do it, and Pet was going to play Pilgrim. In order to make the scene play dramatically, we planned to use a variety of shots and camera angles.

A few days earlier, I'd prepped Pet by laying him down a couple of times, but he's a relaxed horse and getting him to respond wasn't a matter of training as much as just asking him to turn loose and give. We wet him down to make him look sweaty, as though he'd been working real hard, and I started laying him down. It was a piece of cake.

Bob was directing the scene from off camera. After a number of takes I went over to him and said, "You know, this would be a better shot if *you* lay the horse down your-self. You can do it. You don't need me to double for you." Bob was a little unsure. He doesn't make his living working with horses like I do.

I had an idea. I asked the cinematographer, Bob Richard-son, who was in between shots, "Do you want to try to lay the horse down?" Richardson said he would. I said, "Step up here and pull on the horn when I tell you."

Bob was watching, and just as Richardson was about to pull on the saddle horn to lay Pet down, he walked up and said, "Well, if he can do it, I ought to be able to." Note Bob responding to making the right thing easy!

I said, "Give it a try," Richardson stepped aside, and Bob gently laid Pet down. There wasn't anything to it.

Once he was confident that he could do it on camera, Richardson and his crew got the shot set up, and Redford laid the horse down. It was a beautiful shot that worked great because the picture's star performed the action.

The scene became somewhat controversial because many people thought we were being unkind to the horse. Nothing could be farther from the truth. Laying a horse down is a technique I learned from my teachers, and I've used it over the years with horses that are really troubled. Under the right cir-cumstances, it can save a horse's life by helping him into a frame of mind where he can trust the human. In many cases, this will be the first time in his life that he's been able to do so.

When I pick up a front leg, the horse is confined and can't escape. He must begin to trust and not panic so that he doesn't flip over backward and hurt himself. First, he must feel confident to move and then stand. I drive him first on three legs to eliminate the danger for him. It usually takes only a few steps for a horse to get comfortable standing on three legs. I start him off on three legs because a horse lies down with his front feet first. By picking up a front leg, I'm putting the horse in a position where he can think that lying down is okay.

The technique has nothing to do with brute force. I don't throw him down. I work with him by pulling on the saddle horn a little at a time. Every time he gives, I give. Gradually my idea becomes his idea. It occurs to him to relax, give to the rope, and lie down. The closer he gets to the ground, the more relaxed he gets.

A troubled horse may be reluctant at first, but given a little time to search and consider, he will eventually lie down. Usually it doesn't take more than just a couple of minutes. Quite often, it takes no more than a few seconds.

A really troubled or terrified horse is pretty much convinced that the human is a predator. He's pretty sure that when he finally does lie down, he's going to lose the one thing that means everything to him, and that's his life. This moment is the opportunity to go to your horse. As Tom Booker did with Pilgrim in the movie, you can sit with him, rub him, comfort him, and cuddle him. You can show him that even though you have every opportunity, you won't take advantage of him. You're there to be his friend, to be his partner.

© Bill Reynolds

Buck "laying down" a horse.

When the horse lies down and finds that your response is different from what he expected, you have an opportunity to bond that you never could have gotten any other way. Then, after the horse gets up, you have the further opportunity to accomplish things with him without much of the defensive behavior that has inhibited his ability to change.

When people ask me to lay a horse down the way they saw it done in the movie, I decline. Laying down is not a circus sideshow act. It's a valuable tool for helping horses with troubled lives.

It would have been nice if there had been time in the movie to explain that laying Pilgrim down was done to save his life, but as I've said, *The Horse Whisperer* wasn't about teaching people how to work with horses. It was a love story. My own story is about horses, and I guess it's a love story, too. I do the things I do when I work with horses because I just plain love them.

I thought my part was over once the movie was made, but I was wrong. I had to go to New York for the press junket, an event put on by the studio to preview the movie for film critics and the press. The folks at Disney wanted me to be the person from the film to comment on the livestock work—the press wanted to meet a real "horse whisperer."

The movie's publicist, Kathy Orloff, promised she would be there to run interference. She had helped me understand the business of making a movie, filling some gaps in my knowledge. She's a pro from the word go, so I felt much better.

The call to go to New York came right after I finished a clinic near Mammoth, California, so the timing worked. My folks and I had been to New York once, when Smokie and I were guests on the TV show *What's My Line*, with Arlene Francis and Soupy Sales, but that had been a long time ago.

Bill Reynolds and I stayed at the Four Seasons Hotel, a pretty high-dollar deal where rooms came with remote-controlled drapes (I didn't have curtains until I was thirty). Those drapes were the nicest I'd ever seen, even though I thought they needed hemming. They were kind of bunched up on the floor, but Bill said they were supposed to stay that way. He said they called it "puddling." I still don't know how he knew that. I thought that's what a cowdog does when you're too hung over to let him out of the bunkhouse.

My first morning there, I pointed the remote and opened the drapes from twenty feet away. Then I put on my hand-painted cowboy tie with a solid-gold tie bar, a hand-tailored charo-style bolero coat, and a new custom-made felt hat.

The press event was held at another hotel, so Bill and I together with a girl from Disney were escorted to a limousine. It was drizzling rain, and the doormen in front of the hotel held umbrellas over us. I politely said to one of them, "Sir, I appreciate your concern for my headwear, but if a little rain is going to ruin it, it isn't much of a hat." When I realized everyone else was getting the same treatment, I smiled and got into the car.

A press junket is basically a round-robin. You sit in a small room and meet one at a time with folks from the "working press," as they are called (I kept wondering where the nonworking press fit into the deal). One after another they came into my little room and interviewed me on videotape. The stars of the film, including Bob Redford, Kristin Scott Thomas, Sam Neill, and Scarlett Johansson were getting the same treatment in their own little rooms. Keeping us separate was a good way to get all the interviews done at the same time.

Reporters from TV and radio, newspapers and magazines came in, popped a cassette into the video camera, and after a technician got the lights set, they'd ask me questions for ten minutes or so. Then off they'd go to the next little room. Each of them demanded his or her own special lighting. It didn't matter whether they were from a small local TV station or from one of the bigger outlets, they all saw themselves as stars in their own right and seemed to like the opportunity to shout orders at a cameraman or lighting technician.

I'm a cowboy from Wyoming—a title I'm actually rather proud of—and now that I was in the big city, some of the studio people were a little uneasy about how I was going to handle the interviews. This old rube knew that reporters can be like bulldogs and give you a hard time. That's why I find truth to be the best approach. The press finds it refreshing, and you don't have to remember what you've said.

The first news lady in the room told me she had once been a news anchor at one of the local TV stations. She no longer was, but she maintained the attitude that probably got her the anchor job. Seeing that I was a cowboy, she gave me a condescending look, glanced at her watch, checked her schedule, and said, "I certainly hope this isn't your first interview."

I replied, "Ma'am, I sure hope it isn't yours either." And then I said, "I talked more into a microphone by the time I was twenty-five than you will in your entire life. What's your first question?"

By the time her ten minutes were over, the reporter had changed her tune. She liked hearing about the horses, and at that point the studio executives and producers, who were listening to the interview, were satisfied I was going to be able to handle anybody who came along.

Next on my schedule were a couple of young women from MTV and *Rolling Stone* magazine. One of them asked, "What about those poor horses in Central Park? Don't you think it's just awful how they have to pull those heavy carriages around all day?"

I had an answer for that question. "No, I don't," I said, then explained that the Central Park horses are content. Pulling carriages on rubber-rimmed wheels on paved streets is a low-stress job, and the horses are calm and re-laxed, not anxiously laying their ears back or wringing their tails. Plus, these horses get lots of attention and affection from passersby. And horses love attention and affection as much as we do.

The horses that people should be concerned about are the neglected ones that, after the "newness" of ownership wears off, live in box stalls all day. These horses have no purpose, no jobs to do. All they do is eat and make manure. Even prisoners get to exercise more than these horses, and the horses have never done anything wrong. If they had the choice, these horses would choose to be carriage horses rather than stand in their stalls.

The press junket worked out fine. I met people who were genuinely interested in what it's like to be a cowboy today and what it's like to work with horses the way I do. I could tell they enjoyed doing interviews about something that was realistic, and it was a fine experience for everyone.

* * *

Even people who have read the book and seen the movie ask me, Exactly what is a "horse whisperer" anyway? I define the term as a horseman or horsewoman who has the ability to communicate with a horse in a way the average person has little or no way of understanding. Through experience and study, these men and women learn how really sensitive a horse is and how sensitive they need to be to accomplish things with horses.

Ultimately, they learn how little effort is needed. Someone who doesn't know anything about the ways of a horse could be fooled into thinking the approach is all cosmic or mystical. It's not. Anybody can do it who has a passion to do it and has put in enough time. These people are horsemen and horsewomen, not whisperers.

The real benefit of *The Horse Whisperer* is that it helped the audience understand another way of thinking about horses. It's a good way, and if people want to see it as something mystical, that's fine. I like to think that the work Nick Evans and Robert Redford produced helped a lot of horses and a lot of people, and I'd be proud to ride with them again, anytime.

Afterword

I HAD BEEN HURT A FEW TIMES playing volleyball and basketball as a kid, and over the years I'd come off a few horses. The result was bulging discs in my back. Many active men have the same kind of problem by the time they're forty, and they learn to live with back pain. In 1998 I'd had bad sciatica, but I got over it. The pain was kind of gone, and I thought that was the end of it. What I didn't realize was that I still had those bulging discs.

In 1999, I was in Maine starting a two-year-old colt. He was kind of touchy, and when I saddled him he bucked pretty hard. Three or four hours later he was still bucking hard. I got on him the next day, and we got along fairly well. He didn't buck, and I had him walking, trotting, and loping, as well as turning and accepting me swinging a rope on him.

Just as I was about ready to get off, I got a little too close to the round corral fence. The toe of my left boot hung up on a rail, which stretched my leg out behind me. It also drove the heel of my left boot into the colt's flank. He wasn't so solid that he could handle that kind of stress, and he immediately started bucking. With my legs stuck out behind me, I couldn't make much of a bronc ride. The colt bucked me off over his head and into the fence, and I opened a fair-size gash in my scalp.

Furthermore, while I was down, the colt bucked over the top of me and stepped on my back, which broke a couple of my ribs. He also stepped on my hip and my ankle. He missed me with only one foot out of his four.

I hurt pretty bad, and I was a little concerned that a rib had been driven through a lung. But I could breathe all right, and even though I was in pain, I went ahead and finished the clinic.

A couple of days later I went to the hospital in Portland, Maine, to have X rays taken; my lower back was sore, and I wanted to make sure I didn't have a collapsed lung. The doctors didn't seem too concerned about my back, and with my lungs all right, I went back to work, broken ribs, pain, and all.

I tried to be careful getting on and off colts for the next couple of weeks. The pain was indescribable, but people had been planning all year on going to my clinics, and I wasn't going to let them down.

I was in North Carolina a few weeks later, doing the third day of a three-day clinic. I was just finishing up, having already loped maybe ten miles that morning on my first two colts, and I was on my way to get on my last one. The sun was out, the autumn leaves were still on the trees, and as I was walking down to the round corral, I told myself, "You know, I'm feeling about as good as I've felt in a long time." Indeed, I was almost pain-free.

Over the next hour and a half I loped circles in the round corral, explaining what I was doing to the crowd, when the motion of my hips must have hit just the right angle. I felt a little pinch in my back and a kind of tingling feeling down my right leg. I thought that was odd, but I kept on riding.

A couple of minutes later I thought that I had blown my right stirrup. When I looked down and saw that my foot was still in the stirrup, I knew that I was in trouble. A few more seconds, and I couldn't feel my right leg at all.

I stopped the horse, stepped off, and collapsed to the ground. I couldn't support myself. I couldn't lift my right foot, and the only way I could get my right leg to move forward was by grabbing my pants leg and swinging it.

The arrogance of youth led me to believe I was suffering from only a pinched nerve in my back. After a few days it wouldn't be a problem, I was sure; the swelling would go down, and I'd get over it.

The next day I got on a plane and took off for Colorado where I was scheduled to do a clinic at a guest ranch called the C Lazy U near Boulder. When I changed planes in Cincinnati, I found walking very difficult. Worse than that, I had no sense of where my foot was. I always felt sorry for people whose gaits had been altered because they were crippled up for some reason, and now I really understood what they went through. As I grabbed my pants, lifted my leg, and flopped my right foot forward, people stared at me. I felt like a freak.

So, there I was, trying to get to my plane and with a couple of bags to carry. At every step, I had to stop and lift my leg. I was making my way in this fashion along a marble corridor when I fell flat on my face. Fortunately, a man on an electric cart came by, picked me up, and drove me to the gate.

Mary met me at the Denver airport and helped me into the truck. As we drove out to the C Lazy U, I held a bag of ice I had gotten at the airport against my back. Mary looked over with concern, and when it came right down to it, I was worried, too.

When I started the clinic the following day, I thought sitting in a director's chair could get me by. I made it through the day, but by that night the pain was so bad that friends of mine who were riding in the clinic persuaded me to cancel. They were nurses, and they advised me to get an MRI. It was the first time in my career that I had ever canceled a clinic.

Mary drove me down to Boulder where I saw a neurologist. He gave me the MRI, which revealed two herniated discs in my back. I had no idea at the time what that meant. The doctor explained that nerve damage to my spine might possibly cause permanent damage to the motor function of my right foot. Surgery was going to be the only chance to relieve the pain and possibly get back some movement in my leg.

I couldn't have been more shocked. I tried to keep a stiff upper lip, but then it hit me that all the things I'd loved out of life might be over: to play with my child, to teach her how to play basketball or run with her or maybe even ride a horse again. I hobbled out of the doctor's office ahead of Mary, dragged my way to the truck, and cried like I was a little baby again.

I had the surgery, hoping I'd wake up and my foot would work right away. That wasn't the deal. At first nothing much had changed. I was damn sore from the operation, but my foot still didn't work.

They let me out of the hospital after a couple of days, and Mary and I hung around Boulder for a while until I was strong enough to travel. I walked with a cane and dragged my right leg along. My left leg worked fine, but my right leg didn't. Although I wanted to start physical therapy, the doctors asked me to hold off for a while.

I was depressed for a week after we went home. All the strength I'd always shown my family was gone now. Mary was taking care of me, which was never meant to be; I was supposed to be taking care of her and the kids, and I felt like a burden.

Mary drove me to physical therapy where I'd try to lift weights, but the therapy didn't do the muscles down around my foot any good. They weren't getting the message from the nerve. Some muscles higher up in the leg worked, and after months of intense weight lifting and other exercises I reached the point where I could at least walk in a reasonable manner. But the muscles that operate the tendons going down over my ankle still didn't work.

And they still don't. I have no motor function of my lower right leg. I wear a brace under my boot, and the boot has a zipper so I can get my brace in.

I've always been positive, and I haven't given up. I don't know if you can will a nerve to heal. Over the short term, I can assure you that you can't. Over the long term, I'll get back to you on that.

They say nerves heal real slowly. Lots of things about us heal real slowly. I have time. I'm still a relatively young man, and I'm hopeful that I'll get a lot of that function back. But if I don't—hey, I'm riding horses again and giving clinics. Nothing holds me up in my teaching or traveling: I continue to put on tens of thousands of miles each year. Sure, I'm not a hundred percent, but then again I may have never been a hundred percent, anyway.

We're all kind of back to our lives. Right now, I'm sitting in a hotel room in Lexington, Kentucky, getting ready to have dinner with the man who's in charge of the starters at racetracks all over America. He wants me to help him find a way to get race horses in and out of the starting gates so that everyone is a little safer and gets along a little better. He also wants me to help the people who work at the tracks have a little more understanding about how to work with horses.

© Joe Beeler

Buck riding on the Flying C Ranch in Nye, Montana. Every spring, Buck and a group of "hearty" westerners gather at different ranches for a branding put on by Buck's friend Chas Weldon. Buck is in the foreground with Chas facing (near right) *and Bill Reynolds* (far right).

So, while I'm still trying to work at fixing myself, I'm back fixing other problems in the horse world. I can feed my family, and my family's together and they're doing well and thriving. I can't complain a bit. I'm still blessed.

The stories in this book come from what I've learned traveling around the country working with people and their horses, as well as just living life. I hope that some of the stories have made you laugh and some have made you think. Some even may have made you cry. All of that is real healthy.

I hope God blesses all of you the way he's blessed me. He's blessed me with my family and good friends, with the people I've met, with the horses I've ridden, and with the lessons I've learned. Sometime you may see a cowboy in a truck pulling a horse trailer wave at you going down the road. Just wave back, would you? It's probably me.

I continue to soak on things—think about them—and ponder the events that have shaped my life. Hopefully my life's far from over, and maybe someday we can sit together and I can share some little bits of information that will help you in your search for whatever it is you're looking for. And maybe you can share with me. I hope you find meaning in your life, whatever it is.

In life, we don't know why things happen. I believe God is not responsible for the bad things that happen to you. Sometimes I think He's responsible for the good things, but sometimes it's something you shape up for yourself.

I wish you every success that you deserve. Not just if you ride horses, but in all aspects of your life. That's the best I can wish for you. For me, my life's journey has been laid out in front of me. The road may bend out of sight at times, but I know what lies ahead: the faraway horses.